The Global
House Church
Movement

The Global
House Church
Movement

RAD ZDERO, Ph.D.
Co-founder of *House Church Canada*
www.housechurch.ca

William Carey Library
Pasadena, California
www.WCLBooks.com

Published by William Carey Library, P.O. Box 40129, Pasadena, California, USA 91114, Tel: 1-626-720-8210, Fax: 1-626-794-0477

Cover Design by Ben Butler and Rad Zdero
Back Cover Photo of Author by Hanna van Dijk

Bible versions quoted throughout this book:

NIV: Scripture taken from the HOLY BIBLE, NEW INTERNA-TIONAL VERSION ®. Copyright © 1973, 1978, 1984 by International Bible Society. Used by permission of Zondervan Publishing House. All Rights Reserved.

NASB: New American Standard Bible translation. Copyright © 1960, 1962, 1963, 1968, 1971, 1972, 1973, 1975, 1977, by The Lockman Foundation. All rights reserved.

ISBN 0-87808-342-1

Printed in the United States of America

Library of Congress Cataloging in Publication Data
Main entry under title:
The Global House Church Movement
Includes Bibliographical References and Appendices
1. Missions. 2. Evangelism. 3. Biblical Studies. 4. Church History.
Zdero, Radovan (Rad), 1969—

DEDICATION

To all those who went before us in bringing the fires of renewal,
reform, and revival to the church and the planet, especially Paul &
the first Christians, Peter Waldo & the Poor Ones, the first Anabaptist martyrs, George Fox and his Friends, and John Wesley & those
peculiar people called Methodists

To friends and co-labourers who are walking alongside
me in this journey called the house church movement

To the one who saved my neck, who loves me more than I often
realize, and with whom I will spend an awesome eternity indeed,
Jesus Christ

ENDORSEMENTS

This is an excellent, both scholarly and pastoral introduction into the fascinating phenomenon of the housechurch movement. It communicates in a nutshell historical, practical and biblical insights and will serve as a help to those wanting to bridge the cultural gap between the already fledgling housechurch movements in areas like Asia and the astonished Christian West, who finds itself not as a teacher, but as a student again.

Wolfgang Simson
Author of *Houses that Change the World*
DAWN Ministries
GERMANY

***

I found this book so interesting that instead of just glancing though it, I decided to study it. There is a wealth of material in it and anybody seriously contemplating starting a house church must read this book to avoid disappointments.

This will also be an extremely useful book to keep handy to answer questions when confronted either by a genuine seeker or a hardcore traditionalist. This is a scholarly book and all the hard questions have been meticulously studied and answered either biblically or through the pages of history.

Like all other books on this subject, this book does not interfere with the theological foundations but only attacks the traditional structure of the church. The sacred buildings, the professional clergy, the Sunday gatherings, which are the main pillars of the modern church, are all under the hammer. As soon as this extra-biblical baggage is removed, the church will return to the simplicity and effectiveness of the New Testament model of the church.

The stakes are high because the church must fulfill its mandate to disciple the nations, hence the paradigm shift suggested in this book must be taken seriously by all those who are interested in the advancement of the kingdom of God.

Dr. Victor Choudhrie
Ex-surgeon
House Church Strategy Coordinator
INDIA

All I can say is, WOW. If you want a fast reading, clear, concise, contagious, comprehensive, persuasive, visionary, user-friendly, well-researched, and practical compilation and overview of the modern house church phenomenon, Rad's is the book to read. It is refreshing and to the point, dealing with both the Scriptures and practical applications for believers today.

Steve Atkerson
Editor of *Ekklesia: To the Roots of Biblical Church Life*
New Testament Restoration Foundation
USA

***

Rad Zdero's book provides a brilliant understanding of all the basics of that early church that was so dynamic in changing the world of its day. It is well thought out, articulate, and at the heart of what God is doing through his church around the world today.

There is no question in my mind but that the Lord is about to bring in a great harvest as we get closer and closer to his greatly anticipated return. The harvest, however, requires a return to the simple church of the first century. Only in that form can the church multiply at a rate commensurate with the opportunities the Lord is bringing.

Dr. Jim Montgomery
Founder and President
DAWN Ministries
USA

***

Rad Zdero's new book answers many of the questions being raised about the new house churches springing up around the globe. This book is practical, biblically sound, and refreshing. Thank you, Rad, for your contribution to the body of Christ. I highly recommend this book!

Larry Kreider
Director
Dove Christian Fellowship International
USA

***

From China to India, from Africa to Latin American, church growth is happening explosively. Simple church structures, from meetings in homes to meeting under trees have become the norm in many parts of the world. Is there more to this than escape from persecution and lack of available resources?

Rad Zdero draws from his own personal journey, from the scriptures, and from church history to draw a compelling picture of God at work in these simple, non-institutional structures that are emerging around the world. Rapid church planting happens not by accident, but by design. By God's design. And that design is in readily reproducible, economic models of church life that can and do thrive under all conditions, including Western culture. Read this book, and join the revolution that is rapidly overtaking the church in the West.

Drs. Tony and Felicity Dale
Authors of *Simply Church* and *Getting Started*
Editors of *House 2 House Magazine*
USA

***

Ambitious in scope, clear in presentation, radical in implications. Rad Zdero's manifesto informs and challenges Christians everywhere to wake up to the challenge of the emerging global house church movement. Thank you brother for this important contribution to the global house church revolution. Not only have you participated in what God is doing, you've taken the time to pen an apologia to show others the way.

David Garrison
Author of *Church Planting Movements*
Strategy Coordinator
Southern Baptist Convention—International Mission Board
USA

***

I felt privileged to be one of the first to read this book by Rad Zdero. As someone who has been led from leadership in the traditional model of the church to fully embracing the emerging New Testament house church model, I recommend *The Global House Church Movement* to anyone seeking to understand what the emerging movement is all about. The book contains a wealth of information in very readable form. My prayer is that many will read the book and listen to the Spirit as they do that, for the message has the potential to impact many lives and communities for the Kingdom. Do not miss reading this!

Dr. Willie Joubert
House Church Practitioner
Director, Breakthrough Prayer Ministries
CANADA

***

In this thoughtful treatise on the house church movement, Rad Zdero mines the New Testament (particularly the Pauline epistles), church history, and reports of contemporary movements around the world searching for evidence of home based communities of faith and gives the open minded Christian pause to think about where ecclesiology has gone in the past and where it could, should, and perhaps will have to go in the future to adequately respond to our Lord's call to authentic redemptive ministry in the world.

Some readers will find their hearts immediately beating in sync with the book's thesis. Others will see what it proposes as a worthy creative and complimentary parallel approach. Still others may find it threatening and disconcerting. Whatever the case, it's a book worth reading and prayerfully considering.

Keith Elford
Bishop
The Free Methodist Church in Canada
CANADA

***

My test for a non-fiction book is the degree to which it prompts me to act. I don't need more information. My mind is swollen with data. I do need to be knocked out of my complacency. I do need to think outside of my stereotypes. I do need to be inspired to believe more. I remember the first day that I met this rather radical looking engineering student. From my earliest meeting to the present ten years later, Rad has consistently done all of this for me. His book is no exception. I read it and found my zeal to do church was rekindled. In the months that followed I have taken many strides towards practically engaging that enthusiasm. Thanks Rad.

Jeremy Horne
Leader Development
Vision Ministries Canada/The Navigators of Canada
CANADA

CONTENTS

FOREWORD

When you're part of a house church, you're not dabbling in the latest fad, you're moving up to a higher level of life...the kind of life that God intended from the start.

For that kind of upward leap, you want a guide you can count on. And that's exactly Rad.

Don't let his name fool you. Rad is not a radical. He's the most careful writer in the house church field. If you want a fair and balanced picture of what a house church can do for you, you have it in your hands. You can rely on it. And build your future on it.

Unlike me, Rad is not a fire-belching enthusiast who incinerates the old traditional Protestant church with every other breath. He's kind and fair. Yet he shows you with great clarity the stark contrast between exciting, biblical churches meeting in homes vs. the programmed, professionally run, straitjacketed, spectator church you probably grew up in.

He also shows you how to go out and build your own network of house churches. You can rest assured, his advice is grounded in solid experience, which few in this fledgling house church adventure have much of. In fact, this book could not have been written ten years ago by anyone. With this major work, Dr. Zdero has established himself as a credible spokesman for the home church movement.

I especially commend to you chapter five on "Ten Declarations of the Radical Church". That's destined to be reprinted all over the globe for years to come.

Rad covers all the bases for you ... everything you ever wanted to know about house church life ... plus a blizzard of revelations you never knew to ask about.

So dive in with great expectations. You're about to become an expert on the new, Christ-centered, freedom-giving lifestyle that's beginning to sweep across North America.

James H. Rutz
Chairman, Open Church Ministries
www.openchurch.com

ACKNOWLEDGEMENTS

Many thanks to friends and co-labourers who read this manuscript and gave me valuable feedback: Ben 'sweet' Butler, Kim 'okay everybody' Butler, my partner in house church crime Jason Johnston, my philosopher-king friend Geoff Leung, the 'Navigator' Alex Matheson, and my soon-to-be-Ph.D. sister, Jelica Zdero.

A special thank you to Dr. Stanley E. Porter (Professor of New Testament, Principal and Dean of McMaster Divinity College, Hamilton, ON, Canada) for his scholarly review of the chapter entitled "Biblical Foundation: Church, First-Century Style".

A handshake to all those who kindly agreed to cruise these pages and provide words of endorsement, especially to Jim Rutz for spending his valuable time and energy reading the manuscript, giving feedback, and writing such an encouraging foreword.

Ben Butler needs to be singled out for enthusiastically engaging with me in the creative process to produce the book's cover.

My appreciation extends to the fine folks of William Carey Library publishers for time spent, effort made, money invested, and risk taken on this "long shot" book.

Warrior poet Bob Dylan and social prophets U2 provided me with musical and spiritual solace during the book's creation.

The friendship of my sisters and brothers in the emerging regional house church movement has been a constant reminder that there are 'seven thousand' others (1 Kings 19:14-18).

Hanna van Dijk has given me her support, affection, and photography skills during the publication process.

I've also been inspired by the many brave revolutionaries who journeyed along a road less traveled and reminded God's people to get back to the basics of community and mission. They ignited spiritual fires that are still felt today. I tip my hat especially to the first Christians, Waldensians, Anabaptists, Quakers, and Methodists.

Although many folks provided valuable feedback and support, any shortcomings of the book are, of course, of my own making.

1

THE VISION

THE ONCE AND FUTURE CHURCH

DO YOU NEED TO READ THIS BOOK?

There is currently a global shift going on in the church. There is a new Christianity on the horizon. The Spirit of God is birthing the global house church movement. This phenomenon is sweeping across many parts of our planet in places like China, India, and Cuba, to name a few, and is gaining momentum in North America.

Research on missionary work around the globe demonstrates that the most rapidly growing church planting and evangelistic movements today utilize house-sized churches and cell groups. These efforts are outstripping more traditional approaches to evangelism, church growth, and church planting.

Do you consider yourself a Great Commission Christian? Do you have a deep desire to utilize a simple but effective model for reaching the nations for Christ? Do you want to reach your friends and your nation with an approach to church life and church planting that is biblical, simple, natural, inexpensive, duplicatable, intimate, and is a breeding ground for new leaders?

If so, you need to read this book.

It is rooted in biblical principles, historical perspectives, and personal experiences. It offers you practical and strategic steps to help you get involved in changing the world for Christ, starting right in your own backyard.

Because some involved in this movement are doing so merely out of reaction to the flaws of traditional churches, their literature is sometimes overly negative and unbalanced. Therefore, this book provides a biblical, thoughtful, balanced, and yet revolutionary guide for those currently involved in house churches as they seek to live out New Testament-style Christianity. Lastly, the book also doubles as a training manual for current and potential house church leaders with questions and interactive exercises at the end of each chapter for use in a leaders' huddle.

RECAPTURING THE LOST VISION

The Nature of the Church

Picture if you will, spread out all over the city, small living room-sized groups committed to getting to know each other and God. These groups meet primarily in homes, but also in offices, apartments, and meeting rooms on the local university campus. They have become known as 'house churches'.

Rather than one-man shows, meetings are participatory and interactive family-type gatherings where everyone has the opportunity to contribute something. They gather weekly to explore issues of faith, family, the media, culture, suffering, relationships, career, and social action. They may be working on projects, looking at the Bible, praying, crying, eating, sharing the Lord's Supper, baptizing new believers, and playing.

These house churches are not led or hosted by traditional clergy but by average folks who have a deepening love for Christ and other people. They have discovered that the secret of life is to love God and others and to become more like Christ. These folks simply want to rediscover the power and person of Jesus in community and as they engaged in mission, as his early followers did.

No church buildings, professional clergy, highly polished services, or expensive programs are required nor desired.

The Mission of the Church

So powerful have people's experiences with each other and Jesus been, that many neighbours, co-workers, family members, and friends, who may not even believe in God and may be suspicious of church, are chomping at the bit to get in on the action. These groups continually grow and become so big that they multiply themselves into new groups that are strategically placed in new neighbourhoods, commercial and business settings, and educational institutes. The leaders of these groups empower members with training, resources, and prayers, emphasizing a few essentials rather than a long list of requirements in order to reach out to their communities more effectively.

The Boundary of the Church

The unity of the body of Christ is evident to everyone in the way these Christians work together as a single cohesive citywide church. They do not allow denominational boundaries or traditions to prevent partnering together as one citywide body. To network together, these house churches meet house-to-house, organize citywide events for teaching and worship, and/or have a mobile workers that circulate from group-to-group and city-to-city like blood through arteries. Leaders of these groups from across the city also meet regularly as a team to pray, exchange resources, and coordinate their efforts to strategically plant new house churches—new lighthouses of hope—in every neighbourhood of their city, like yeast working its way through and saturating dough.

The Expansion of the Church

As new leaders emerge and are released to follow their calling to start new multiplying house churches and move like circuit riders from city-to-city, without even knowing it, they are swept up into a movement—their movement, God's movement—which will touch many generations to come. This is part of an emerging reformation of the church in their generation, an underground revolution of faith that will transform their city and blaze across their region, their nation, and the uttermost parts of the earth.

WHAT IS A HOUSE CHURCH?

Some readers may be asking, what exactly is a house church, anyway? There are some surface similarities—such as size and location—between home cell groups that are part of traditional churches on the one hand and New Testament style house churches on the other. But, there is also a vast ocean of difference that needs to be recognized.[1]

---

[1] see *Appendix 1* for a more detailed description of the difference between the first two models of church commonly used and the New Testament house church model.

Traditional Churches

More conventional churches can be pictured as 'cathedral' churches where the home prayer or Bible study group is merely an optional appendage. These home groups usually involve only people who are members of the mother congregation and are not outreach focused. There are usually a few of these small groups floating around, but they are not the main program offered by the congregation. The main thing is the large group Sunday morning service. This is like a bicycle wheel hub (Sunday morning large group) with the odd spoke (home group) protruding out. It can be described as a 'church *with* small groups'.

Cell Churches

Although there is much in common between them, a house church is not even a cell group, which belongs to a larger system involving a pyramid leadership structure with a senior minister at the top. Cell groups are typically outreach focused and normally will grow within a year to the point of multiplying into two groups. In cell churches, there is an equal emphasis on home cell group meetings and traditional Sunday morning worship services. This can be depicted as a hub with many spokes jutting outward from it. This arrangement can be described as a 'church *of* small groups'.

New Testament-style House Churches

This clustering of people is different from both traditional congrega-tions—which have a building, professional clergy, expensive programs, and the main Sunday morning service—and cell churches dotting our Western landscape. House churches are an attempt to get back to the form and function of apostolic Christianity. Stated positively, they are fully functioning churches in themselves, with the freedom to partake of the Lord's Supper, baptize, marry, bury, exercise discipline, and chart their own course. They are volunteer-led and meet in house-sized groups for participatory and interactive meetings involving prayer and worship, Bible study and discussion, mentoring and outreach, as well as food and fun. Because they are typically autonomous, they more easily adapt to persecution, growth, and change, but are also more vulnerable to bad theology and behavior. So, house churches become part of peer networks for health and growth, like a spider web of interlocking strands.

Consequently, house churches can be explained by the principle that 'church *is* small groups.'

A GROWING GLOBAL REVOLUTION

Believe it or not, what you have just read above is basically a description of what the early church of the first three centuries was like; it was a 'living room' movement. This was the church that "upset the world" (Acts 17:6, NASB) in the first century and that forced the mighty Roman Empire to legalize Christianity after a three hundred year showdown. It is also the church that tens of millions of Christians are rediscovering today in places like China, India, Africa, Cambodia, Cuba, England and Western Europe, and, yes, even in North America. Some traditional congregations are even beginning to sell their buildings and reorganize as a web of house churches to more effectively penetrate segments of their city with the great news of Jesus Christ.

During Missionfest Toronto—a Christian trade show where denominations, missions groups, seminaries, and other ministries promote their work—our house church network had a booth with the title banner reading, 'Houses that Change the World: Join the Worldwide House Church Movement'. A visitor to our booth observed that we were really selling an idea to the Christian public. He was right. We were the only group there that was not promoting an organization, but rather a vision, a concept, an idea, a movement. And that's exactly what this book is about. It is about trying to recapture the lost vision of what the Christian church once was, what many are rediscovering today, and how it could function even more biblically and effectively to reach the billions around the world who have not yet personally encountered Jesus Christ. If this vision excites you, dear reader, as much as it excites me, then the following pages should prove to be a very stimulating journey.

My hope and prayer is that God will use this manifesto to shake and shift your paradigms, challenge you to become a spiritual revolutionary, and intelligently and practically coach you in joining the worldwide house church movement as it changes this planet for Christ. To those brave souls who choose to pick up this torch, I salute you. Godspeed.

QUESTIONS FOR GROUP REFLECTION

1. *The Big Picture.* What part of the 'Recapturing the Lost Vision' section excited, concerned, or confused you?

2. *Organizing the Church.* Can you explain the organizational difference between a traditional church, cell-group church, and house church? What do you think are the pros and cons of each?

3. *Linking House Churches Together.* What are three ways described in this chapter in which the house churches of a network can be linked together? Can you think of any other possibilities?

GROUP EXERCISE

Can you see the difference? Break your discussion group into three smaller groups. Each group is responsible to draw a diagram that describes the organizational nature either of a traditional church, a cell church, or a New Testament-style house church network. Come back together and take turns explaining your diagram to the other two groups.

2

PERSONAL EXPERIENCES

MY JOURNEY ALONG THE ROAD LESS TRAVELED

Stories. We crave them because they connect the three strands of past, present, and future into one strong cord we can hang our entire weight from. Some challenge us. Some comfort us. Some are exciting, while others are pretty ordinary. But, each story is unique. I'd like to tell you about the stops I've made along my own road toward the global house church movement.

ENCOUNTERING CHRIST AND HIS PEOPLE

I was born in Canada in 1969 and raised in a nominal Christian environment in the Serbian Orthodox Church. My immigrant parents, though, instilled in me a belief in God, prayer, and personal moral responsibility. But God was still just a vague idea.

When I was fifteen my younger sister brought home a pocket New Testament that she got at school from the Gideon Bible Society. Over the next year, as I read about the life, teachings, death, resurrection, and claims of Christ, I made a decision to surrender the rest of my life to following him. No bells. No whistles. No skywriting. My sister also made the same decision at about that time. This created some serious tensions at home with the folks, to the point where we had to read the Bible and pray very secretively in our rooms. My parents were worried that we'd go crazy or join some sort of cult.

During the next few years, I never attended an evangelical church due to family circumstances. But, there were some Christian TV shows that I watched and some fellow Christian students at my highschool. There were about six of us who used to get together every week for a small group Bible study, the next three years being very foundational for me. One of the main lessons I learned during this time was my need for some form of Christian community to empower me to follow Christ more closely.

EARLY UNIVERSITY YEARS

In 1987, I enrolled at McMaster University in Hamilton, Canada. I immediately got plugged in with the Campus Crusade for Christ (CCC) group where I was challenged to grow in my personal prayer life and in personal evangelism. The CCC staff guy, Dave, intentionally discipled me over the next two years in a one-on-one and small group context, imparting to me a vision for how God could use my life for something bigger. I definitely consider him one of my three spiritual fathers. At the same time I was building an evangelistic small group on the side with a few other classmates, some Christian, some not.

As CCC in Canada reorganized itself in the late 1980s, they shut down their ministry at McMaster, so I got involved with the Navigator group in 1989. For the next four years Don—who was the Navigator staff guy and my second spiritual dad—deliberately mentored me one-on-one, challenged me to get involved with and eventually lead a men's Bible study, and invited me to join the Navigator student leadership team. On the side, because of my evangelistic bent, I was still carrying on an evangelistic Bible study with some classmates.

I also attended the monthly student led worship services held in one of the campus pubs and even visited some local churches my friends attended on Sunday mornings. For the most part these visits were okay experiences. After a while, though, I started to lose interest because of their overly emotional nature, their foreign 'Christian-ese' jargon and music, and the passive nature of simply attending.

HOUSE CHURCH ON CAMPUS

In 1993, I moved to Kingston, Canada, to attend Queen's University to pursue doctoral studies, also continuing my involvement with the existing Navigator group there. Jeremy, my third spiritual dad and the national campus director for the Navigators, came to visit and invited me to come on officially as associate Navigator staff and team up with the current staff couple at Queen's.

Over the next few years, every Thursday night would see fifty students cram into the living room and kitchen of a house by the campus. We'd spend the first forty-five minutes worshipping God through song and music. Someone would give a short message or testimony about what Jesus was doing in their lives, followed by a few organizational announcements. Then for the next ninety minutes we'd break into about seven or eight small groups in various rooms of the house for interactive Bible study, prayer, discussion, and lots of laughter. We'd funnel back into the living room and kitchen at the end of the evening for food and socializing. There were always a few non-Christian friends and classmates who would come out and visit or participate in one of the introductory Bible studies. Those were exciting times!

These people were my friends, my spiritual community, my church. This was clear to me, but not to everyone. People sometimes asked me which church I attended. My response was always two-fold. I often started by saying I didn't 'go' to church but, rather, I 'was' the church. God's spirit lived in me and, as a temple of the Holy Spirit, there was no need for me to go to a building on Sunday mornings. Then, after thoroughly confusing my conversation partner and making them suspect I was some sort of heretic, I would assure them that I was indeed part of a church. The Navigator group functioned like a church for me, although it didn't look like the traditional version because it met in someone's home.

Three vital things were firmly established in my mind at the end of these university years. First, much of evangelical Christianity, as with any other group, is permeated with certain jargon, music, dress codes, and behaviors, that aren't necessarily relevant to or part of the core message of Christ. These are dispensable secondary items. Second, small groups are vital for the growth of Christians and an effective tool for reaching non-Christians. Third, simply attending a conventional local church on Sunday mornings was absolutely unnecessary as long as I was actively participating in some form of authentic Christian community.

CELL GROUPS IN A TRADITIONAL CHURCH

In 1999, I finished my doctorate and began to work with my research group as a scientific writer, editor, and project coordinator. After years of involvement on the campus with the Navigators, I felt the need to transition out of that scene. Into what, I didn't exactly know. During that summer of decision, I had an independent home group of students meeting at my apartment for weekly spiritual discussions and got my hands on some house church books and articles. At the same time, a friend of mine invited me to a brand new local church that he said was anything but typical, except that it had a building. I was, to say the least, skeptical. After checking it out over a few months and participating in anything and everything that was going on, I made a decision to get seriously involved.

For the next two years, my job was to get the cell (or small) group ministry going. I was apparently the cell group guru of our church, helping to start and/or organize up to eleven cell groups at one point, some healthier than others. During this time I met Jason, an assistant pastor of a partnering church in town who, coincidentally, was trying to get cell groups going in his church. After a few chats, we felt it would be great to bring the leaders of these cell groups from both churches together for monthly leadership training times, which we did for the next ten months. As we worked, talked, discovered, and prayed together, we felt a real convergence in our visions for how the ideal church could function and be organized.

Our growing conviction was that cell groups were indispensable building blocks of a church intent on developing community and engaging in mission. Jason's church did not share this vision and viewed the emerging cell groups as merely one program among many. Most of the people in my church, although much more progressive in many ways, were still unsure of what the role of cell groups really was.

I knew I had to talk to my two friends, who were the pastors, about what direction we were going as a church. At the risk of insulting them, I brought a bowl of fruit salad and a bunch of grapes into one of our weekly morning meetings to symbolically demonstrate the role of cells. I explained that the fruit salad was like a traditional church that had all sorts of programs going on—the youth group, the women's missionary fellowship, the clothing bank, the Sunday morning service, etc.—cell groups being only one of many options. The fruit salad was a church 'with' cell groups. The bunch of grapes, however, was like a cluster of cell groups. There were no other programs. All of ministry—teaching, worship, nurture, accountability, friendships, evangelism, and service—was done in and through the cells.

Although I assured them I really believed God could use both models, I needed to know personally where the church was going, because my passion was for grapes. Were our visions the same? It turned out they were not. That was fine for me, and there were no hard feelings. The clarity was very freeing for me. I just needed to know. Months later, when it came time to leave, I was given a great send off by this church and formally commissioned as a house church missionary to Toronto. My personal friendships are still strong with many in that church; some of my best friends are there.

From this experience I learned a few more things. First, it is very tough for an entire group of people to undergo a significant paradigm shift in one area, regardless of how progressive they might be in another. Moving a traditionally structured church towards a cell church—not to even mention dropping the building and reorganizing as a network of biblical house churches—will not come without years of toil. It is almost impossible. Only making a few changes here and there is just a band-aid solution and doesn't get to the root. It is better to start from complete scratch. That is exactly what we have done.

Second, traditional churches that are mission minded would do well to recognize that there are potential church planters in their midst. Churches can commission them to take on this task, releasing them to start house churches in their city for the sake of kingdom growth.

Third, during this time, I also underwent a rapid and major shift in my thinking regarding what the most strategic church structure looked like in light of my personal experiences, a study of New Testament patterns, and exponential church growth in the world today. Specifically, I moved from a traditional mindset ('church *with* small groups') to a cell-group church model ('church *of* small groups') to an understanding of New Testament-style house church networks ('church *is* small groups').

LAYING THE FOUNDATION

In 2001, I finally moved to the Toronto area with Jason and a few other people with the intention of planting a cell-based church. However, the more we read and talked and experienced, the more we recognized that what we were really talking about was house church networks. We did not foresee a building, school gym, or community centre being at the heart of what God was asking us to do. We wanted to go back to the simplicity and power of the early Christians we read about in the New Testament.

Several years back after going for a long late night walk, I went home and began praying fervently about direction for the work that God was calling us to. While in prayer, I was strongly impressed to read a specific scripture, namely Isaiah 27:2. It flashed across my mind. I had absolutely no clue what the content of the passage was since I had not read through Isaiah in a long while. So, I went to the passage and read it: "In that day, a vineyard of wine, sing of it!" (NASB). Or, as another version renders it, "In that day sing about a fruitful vineyard" (NIV). A few lines later, the passage continues: "In the days to come Jacob will take root, Israel will blossom and sprout, and they will fill the whole world with fruit." (Isaiah 27:6, NASB). Needless to say, I was deeply moved by that little prayer time and felt that the Spirit was confirming to me that something big was about to unfold, and I had the privilege of partnering with God in some small way. Since then, I've had unusual confirmations in the form of specific dreams, phrases impressed on my mind, and pictures that I believe are from God, to encourage me to keep stepping through the doors he's been opening.

But, what has happened since that late night prayer time two years back?

As a fledgling neighbourhood house church, we started with about nine adults and two kids gathering weekly in a home for open and interactive meetings involving worship, prayer, Bible study, the Lord's Supper, food, and fun. We knew a few Christians in the area and began to invite some others to join us. We have had several people come and go because, despite an initial desire to belong, some folks just could not emotionally make the shift away from their traditional church experience.

But, it is more than just a weekly meeting. Our group is really about being an authentic 24-hour, 7-day-a-week, Christian community living the common life together and reaching out to those around us. The initial prototype house church has grown and meets together Sunday evenings and at other times during the week, with a few other friends who may be preparing to join in.

Evangelistically, we also have made some strong friendships with non-Christians through work, school, the neighbourhood, and a local drop-in centre. A number of these have joined us for a mid week 'Introduction to Christianity' dinner and discussion group we host in our homes. Some of these friends are making significant steps forward to Christ. We are hoping to eventually transition them into the house church. Last summer, we had our first baptisms in a backyard pool, one of the girls having only recently come to faith. We have also used one of the free community kiosks at the nearby mall—the largest one in the province—to set up a display and engage interested people in conversation about faith issues. Lastly, to address some material needs in the community, we have volunteered some time at a local drop-in center, helped out at a local food bank, and participated in 'Operation Christmas Child'.

From our calling to see a house church movement emerge in our region, we hosted an information night at our home for the broader Christian community in our city and the few home churches in the region. The initial face-to-face contact with other house churches was the first step in the establishment of a regional work. Some of these house churches are freelance while others, like us, are connected with a larger denomination. We have covenanted with several of these home churches, which entails a more intensive working relationship than with the others. Especially through our website and word of mouth, we have also made contact with a number of people internationally, nationally, and locally who are very interested in the house church movement. We have met with a number of these folks to answer questions, given them some practical advice on how to get going and growing, and equipped them with resources. Some are taking steps to starting new house churches.

Our initial prototype house church (at the time of this writing), has released me to spin off a second home church, which is now off and running with a whole new crew of people in my neighbourhood. We have also helped two other groups get going, with whom we have continued a close relationship. So, our particular network includes four functioning house churches spread over three cities. As a result of these efforts in partnership with others, the emerging house church movement in our region involves home churches and networks in twenty cities and counting. We are also actively involved in participating in the emerging house church phenomenon on the national scene through various consultation groups, communication channels, and conferences.

Finally, it has been clear to me that what is going on in North America is a fledgling house church trend. It is not yet a movement. Those of us immersed in this are certainly at the fringe of the Christian community; it is the road less traveled. It does not seem like much now, but the explosive potential is there. As I survey the immensity of what Jesus is doing globally through the house church movement today, I am gripped by the awesome vision of what the church in North America could become in the years ahead. Sometimes, in communicating vision to people, I like to phrase it this way: "Every Church, Start a Church, Every Year". In the next ten years, this could mean the birth of 1000 house churches in our region. So, for this fellow at least, the future is here!

QUESTIONS FOR GROUP REFLECTION

1. *Paradigm Shifts.* What major shifts in your thinking have you experienced in your life, work, or ministry over the years?

2. *More Shifts.* What further shifts—emotional, intellectual, or circumstantial—were or are major barriers from get fully involved with the house church movement?

3. *Small Groups Rule.* What influences have small groups and cell groups had in your spiritual formation? What, if any, personal needs were not met for you in these groups that could have been addressed if they were full-fledged New Testament-style house churches?

GROUP EXERCISE

Paradigm Shifts. In your large group or break out groups, take any one object (e.g. pencil, coin, glass, scissors, etc.) and place it in the center of the table. Brainstorm together about different ways of describing what the object actually is. For example, a coin could be described as currency, a flat disc, a metal cookie, a circle, a wheel, a robot's teardrop, etc. This should illustrate the idea that an object can be many different things other than what we normally assume, if we are willing to begin thinking out-of-the-box.

3

BIBLICAL FOUNDATIONS

CHURCH, FIRST-CENTURY STYLE

For many of us today, the word 'church' elicits images of a special man running a special service in a special building on a special day for a special fee. Or, it might bring to mind things like boards, denominations, organizations, or those who serve as full-time clergy. Because this pattern has existed for the past 1700 years within most Christian traditions, it may come as a shock to find out that Christians in the first century gathered, organized, and thought of themselves in a very different way. They would have found what is considered church today, especially as it appears in the West, quite foreign.

The purpose of this chapter is to examine the New Testament for evidence of any deliberate first-century pattern set out by Jesus and the apostles for church *function* and *form*. Specifically, this chapter explores the following seven key questions: (1) How did the early Christians view themselves? (2) Where did the early church meet? (3) What were first-century churches like? (4) What about leadership in the early church? (5) How were churches connected as a movement? (6) How did the early church grow? (7) Did the apostles expect churches to follow their blueprint? We now turn to the church, first-century style.

1. HOW DID THE EARLY CHRISTIANS VIEW THEMSELVES?

The first issue that must be addressed is how the early Christian community understood itself in relation to its Lord and the world around it. Although not an exhaustive list by any means, the following are some of the key ideas found in the New Testament that permeated the mindset of the first Christians that, in turn, determined how they practically organized themselves and functioned. In other words, their beliefs determined their behavior, their function determined their form, their mandate determined their method. Let us now turn to some of the more significant ways they described and understood themselves.

The Assembly

Probably the most common imagery evoked in the New Testament is that described by the Greek word 'ekklesia', appearing 114 times. This word, meaning 'assembly' or 'meeting', is the word translated as 'church'. The three main uses of 'church' in the New Testament are in reference to believers gathering in someone's home[2], the citywide or regional church[3], and the universal church.[4] The word is *never* used in reference to a special building, a religious ceremony, or a class of paid professional leaders. This would have been incomprehensible to the early Jesus movement. This particular word brings out the importance of clustering, assembling, or meeting together as believers.

The Discipleship Circle

This image is that of a circle of people gathered around Christ. Although at times there was a throng of people following Jesus along the dusty roads of Palestine, he chose a small group of twelve disciples in particular to be with him. It was with these that he spent the majority of his time, training them so that they would become capable leaders in their own right, able to train others also. In the words of scripture, "he appointed twelve, that they might be with him, and that he might send them out."[5] Jesus also promised that "where two or three come together in my name, there am I with them."[6] By defining his inner circle and suggesting he was present

---

[2] Acts 2:26, 5:42, 12:12, 16:14-15, 20:20; Rom 16:3-5; 1 Cor 16:19; Col 4:15-16; Philem 1:2

[3] Acts 9:31; Rom 1:7; 1 Cor 1:2; 2 Cor 1:1; Gal 1:2; Eph 1:1; Philip 1:1; Col 1:1; 1 Thes 1:1

[4] Mat 16:18; 1 Cor 12:28, 15:9; Eph 1:22, 3:10-11, 5:22-32; Heb 12:23

[5] Mark 3:14 (NASB)

[6] Matt 18:20 (NIV)

whenever believers met, Jesus encouraged the early Christian communities to see him at their center when they gathered.

The Bride of Christ

The next metaphor is brought to our attention by the apostle Paul, who wrote that the mysterious bond between Christ and the church is revealed in the relationship between husband and wife. The dynamic is one punctuated by love and submission.[7] John the Baptist[8] and the writer John[9] also made explicit use of this imagery to describe Christ and the church, with Jesus giving possible allusion to it in the parable of the wedding feast.[10]

The Body of Christ

Another powerful visual that Paul invoked several times is that of the church as Christ's body.[11] This implies a living, organic, and mutually dependent relationship between the two. Just as a headless body is lifeless and cannot function, so too is a head useless on its own unless it has a body that will do its bidding. Paul emphasizes that as Christ gives direction to his body, its component parts, i.e. believers, are to be united in purpose. They are also to recognize and celebrate the function of different parts of that body. Thus, this metaphor speaks of two primary functions the church saw as important: unity among believers and the equal opportunity aspect of mutual ministry.

The Family of God

The writings of the apostles are riddled with familial references to the church in family terms. References are made to the family of God, little children, God's household, brothers, sisters, and children of God, with God himself being the heavenly father.[12] This emphasis was something first century believers could easily relate to because of the strong family bonds and legal ties that characterized Mediter-

---

[7] Eph 5:22-32
[8] John 3:29
[9] Rev 18:23, 19:7, 21:2, 21:9, 22:17
[10] Luke 14:12-23
[11] Rom 7:4; 1 Cor 10:16-17, 12:4-30; Eph 4:11
[12] John 1:12-13; Eph 2:19; Gal 6:10; 1 Tim 3:4-5,15, 5:1-2; Heb 2:11; 1 Pet 4:17; 1 John 2:1,12-14, 3:1; 2 John 1:1

ranean society.[13] This image emphasized the important function of having boundaries that clearly defined membership in the community.

A Spiritual Temple

The apostle Peter characterized believers as living stones fitted together to form a spiritual house for God's good pleasure. This spiritual house was a place where a holy priesthood, i.e. all believers, offers up spiritual sacrifices to God.[14] The use of this imagery was certainly a deliberate ploy on Peter's part. He knew that it would remind Jewish converts to Christianity of the stone Temple in Jerusalem and the animal sacrifices that were carried out there for hundreds of years by a select priestly caste. By using this illustration, Peter implicitly suggested an end to the notion that God lived inside physical structures. The Jewish Temple system was now at an end. Rather, a new era had been ushered in characterized by true spiritual worship of God unrestricted by 'holy' locations, something predicted by Jesus and vigorously affirmed by Stephen the first martyr.[15]

Other Word-Pictures and Terms

Lesser-employed word pictures include vine and branches, teacher and pupil, a chosen race, kingdom of God, a royal priesthood, a holy nation, a people for God's inheritance, soldiers, and a shepherd and his flock.[16] These images speak of identity, relationship, community, and mission, each of which is an important aspect of living out the Christian life.

* * *

But, how did the early church live this out practically from day to day as it engaged in community and mission? How did it organize itself as a movement? Specifically, how did its beliefs about the important functions it was meant to carry out determine the specific forms it developed to do so. As we shall see, *the early church minimized the complexity of its forms in order to maximize the effectiveness of its functions.*

---

[13] Acts 11:14, 16:15,31, 18:8; see Joseph Hellerman, *The Ancient Church as Family*, Minneapolis: Fortress Press, 2001.
[14] 1 Pet 2:5
[15] John 4:20-24, Acts 7:46-50
[16] Luke 9:62, 17:21; John 13:13, 15:1-8; Acts 20:28; 1 Pet 5:2; Eph 6:10-17

2. WHERE DID THE EARLY CHURCH MEET?

Privately from House to House

The gospels report that homes—among other places—were a natural part of Jesus' life and ministry. Christ was worshipped as a baby in a house,[17] he healed Peter's mother-in-law at home,[18] the Last Supper was held in a house,[19] and Jesus preached to people crowded into homes.[20] Christ also trained his disciples during a hands-on assignment by sending them out in pairs to preach from village to village. They were instructed to find a 'man of peace' in each village that was responsive to their message and build a spiritual base of operations from that home.[21]

Private homes also had a pivotal role in the life of the early church. Shortly after Pentecost, the apostle Peter and the Jerusalem church began a pattern of meeting daily from house to house, living a common life together which was characterized by eating meals, praying, sharing goods, and holding to the apostles' teachings.[22] Peter also brought the message of Christ to the Roman officer Cornelius' friends and family who were gathered in his home.[23] Sometime later, during a very severe systematic persecution of the church in Jerusalem, Saul of Tarsus was reported to have gone from house-to-house searching for believers and likely barging in during the middle of church meetings.[24] Later, as a Christian convert Saul (now known as the apostle Paul) embarked on his missionary travels across the Roman Empire, regularly clustering believers into homes and ending his letters by greeting those who hosted these gatherings.[25] The apostle John warns his readers not to welcome false teachers into their homes, referring most probably to house church

---

[17] Mat 2:11
[18] Mat 8:14-16
[19] Mat 26:18
[20] Mark 2:1
[21] Luke 10:1-11
[22] Acts 2:46, 5:42, 12:12
[23] Acts 10
[24] Acts 8:3
[25] Acts 16:14-15,29-34, 20:6-8,20; Rom 16:3-5; 1 Cor 16:19; Col 4:15-16; Philem 1:2

gatherings rather than mere social occasions.[26] These house churches were spread across the empire in cities like Jerusalem, Ephesus, Colossae, Corinth, Laodicea, Troas, Philippi, and Rome.

We do not know for certain that all believers everywhere in the first century met *exclusively* in homes. But, what can be said is that the early church met *primarily* in homes for believers' meetings and even some evangelistic efforts. Consequently, it can accurately be described as a house church movement.

What about Public Places?

There were, though, other more public places where believers were sometimes to be found. What do we make of the fact that Christians were spotted—sometimes in large groups—in places like the Temple courts in Jerusalem and in synagogues?[27] Is this inconsistent with an otherwise seemingly clear pattern of home meetings? Not if things are understood in their proper context.

Because the first Christians were ethnically Jewish, they would have found it very natural to continue being part of Jewish religious life by meeting in the Temple courts and in synagogues,[28] even after believing in Jesus. However, a close look at these biblical accounts shows that these public places were used primarily for evangelistic endeavors—characterized by preaching and/or healing—carried out by Jewish Christians for the purpose of drawing fellow Jews to faith in Christ. They would continue in this fashion until they were ousted or gained converts whom they would then invite into a home setting.[29] In one specific situation, Paul was actually barred from continuing his evangelistic preaching in a synagogue and was forced to rent a lecture hall where he could continue the same kind of work.[30] As such, these events cannot be properly understood as

---

[26] 2 John 10

[27] Acts 2:1-3:26, 5:12-16, 13:14-16, 14:1-7, 16:13-18, 17:1-5, 18:4,24-28

[28] Archaeological and literary evidence suggests that even first-century synagogues may have been private homes—with some exceptions like Luke 7:1-5—opened up to the local Jewish public for prayer, Bible reading, and sharing a meal on the Sabbath (see Richard Ascough, *What are they saying about the formation of Pauline churches?* Mahwah, New Jersey: Paulist Press, 1998, pp.12-14).

[29] Acts 18:4-8

[30] Acts 19:8-10

believers' meetings in which mutual encouragement in the faith was the main purpose, but were rather used for evangelism.

Thus, public places like the Temple courtyard and synagogues were gathering places customarily used as forums for outreach, but did not rival the house-to-house practice for church meetings. Any apparent attachment to sacred buildings was a temporary, transitional, and solely Jewish Christian experience. The previous role of sacred buildings was now at an end and no longer part of God's plan, as predicted by Jesus and confirmed by the first martyr Stephen.[31] This out-of-the-box living faith was now being lived out by Christian communities, especially outside Palestine, in the very ordinary environment of people's homes and in their communities.

Circumstantial Reasons for Meeting in Homes?

The apostolic pattern of meeting primarily in homes occurred in a particular political and cultural context. The church undoubtedly needed to negotiate various social forces, which were bound to affect the way it lived out its mandate. Some natural questions arise: What about the persecution and poverty that swirled around the first-century Christians? Or, maybe the ancient disciples simply went through a temporary house church phase they knew they would outgrow later on. Perhaps, if they had the freedom and money, they would have constructed special church buildings? Aren't these the real reasons why it was a house church movement? These are legitimate questions that deserve to be addressed.

First, a popular but inaccurate notion is that the first-century church was systematically and continually persecuted and had to meet secretly in homes; they had no other choice. However, to the contrary, any reputable history textbook will point out that large systematic persecution in that period was sporadic and localized, occurring on only four separate occasions: Saul of Tarsus was instrumental in a 'great persecution' of Christians in Jerusalem in about 35 A.D.[32] which involved a house-to-house search; the Roman Emperor Claudius exiled Jews and Christians from Rome in 49 A.D.[33]; the Emperor Nero arrested and tortured believers in Rome in

---

[31] John 4:21-24; Acts 7:46-50
[32] Acts 8:1-4, 9:1-2
[33] Compare ancient Roman historian Suetonius, *Life of Claudius* (25.4), with Acts 18:2

64 A.D.[34]; the Emperor Domitian persecuted Christians in Rome and Asia Minor in the mid 90's A.D.[35] Most of the oppression mentioned in the New Testament was at the hands of unruly mobs, limited to one locality, and directed at specific individuals (e.g. Peter, John, Stephen, Paul)[36] rather than at the entire church as such. At other times, Christians actually enjoyed good rapport with their neighbours, as occurred in the early days of the church in Jerusalem and later in the regions of Judea, Galilee, and Samaria.[37]

Second, poverty as a major cause for believers meeting in homes is also often proposed. Similar to the mistaken idea of systematic persecution is the mistaken idea of pervasive poverty. Certainly, there were many churches and individuals who were indeed in material need, e.g. the Jerusalem church.[38] However, other Christians were of some societal position and/or wealth like the Ethiopian royal official, Cornelius the Roman officer, Lydia the merchant, Erastus the city treasurer, possibly some relatives or associates of Rome's Emperor himself, Philemon the slave owner, and various other anonymous wealthy Christians.[39] If church buildings were important these individuals could have brought together some finances to get a building program going as did a Roman officer in Jesus' day, who built a synagogue for a local Jewish community.[40] However, no such biblical or archaeological record of church structures has been found whatsoever for the first century.

Third, it has been suggested that house churches were perhaps only a temporary phase in the development and growth of early Christianity; the apostles probably expected Christians to eventually use dedicated buildings at some future point. This idea, though, is at

---

[34] See ancient Roman historian Tacitus, *Annals* (15.44).
[35] C.C. Richardson (ed.), *Early Christian Fathers*, New York: Collier Books, 1970, pp.34,37; see also Rev 1:9-11 which speaks of the apostle John and the churches in Asia Minor experiencing persecution in the mid 90's AD.
[36] Acts 4:13-23, 5:18, 6:8—7:60, 12:1-18, 19:23-41
[37] Acts 2:46-47, 5:12-16, 9:31
[38] Gal 2:10
[39] Acts 8:26-39, 10:1-2, 16:14, 17:4; Romans 16:23; Philip 4:22; Philemon 1:16; 1 Tim 6:17; James 5:1-6
[40] Luke 7:1-5

odds with the fact that they continued this way for nearly three hundred years. The early believers were one of the few religious groups at the time that did not make use of some sort of sacred buildings or structures. This stands in stark contrast to the Greeks and Romans, who dedicated temples to their gods, and the Jews, who had their Temple in Jerusalem. The earliest archaeological evidence of any Christian structures comes from the third century, when a private home along the River Euphrates seems to have been altered to accommodate a group of about one hundred people.[41] However, this example is certainly not representative of first-century custom and was the exception rather than the rule even in the third century. It was not until the early fourth century, as the Emperor Constantine started pumping money into the newly legalized Christian religion, that Christianity first collectively owned real estate.

In conclusion, persecution, poverty, and an early developmental stage were not necessarily deciding factors for the phenomenon of home meetings. Rather, other considerations, like their theology of the church as family, living out community life together, and the interactive nature of church meetings led them to meet in homes. In other words, the early church did not consciously utilize or explicitly advocate the house church structure because of its efficiency and effectiveness. Rather, the house church form was simply the natural result of their beliefs and values as modeled and initiated by the apostles.

3. WHAT WERE FIRST-CENTURY CHURCHES LIKE?

What were New Testament-style house churches like? What exactly did Christians do in believers' meetings? How did Christians in these house churches contribute to one another's lives as they did 'life together'? Were there essentials commonly found in most or all house churches in the first century?

In the following, the format of church meetings will first be examined followed by a detailed look at the mystical, intellectual, spectacular, symbolic, relational, evangelistic, material, temporal, and sociological elements that characterized house churches.

---

[41] Steve Atkerson, *Toward a House Church Theology*, Atlanta: New Testament Restoration Foundation (www.ntrf.org), 1998, pp.33-34.

The Open Format of Church Meetings

What were first century church meetings like? Were they liturgical, charismatic, evangelistic, or teaching-centered? There are answers to these questions, since we do have clear guidelines as to the format and purpose of church gatherings. Although there is no detailed play-by-play account of a believers' get-together, there are several important passages that outline the two primary operating principles that guided the wide open format of meetings and church life in general: participation and interaction.

Participation refers to the process of everyone having the chance to give something to the group. Rather than a religious service being run by a few active participants for a group of rather passive onlookers, everyone had ample opportunity and the responsibility to use their God given capacities and skills. Everyone was encouraged to participate and bring to the 'spiritual table' whatever contribution they could. After a very lengthy discussion on the purpose and nature of believers' meetings, the apostle Paul summarizes the Spirit-led and equal opportunity format as follows:

> What then shall we say, brothers? When you come to-gether, *everyone* has a hymn, or a word of instruction, a revelation, a tongue or an interpretation. All of these must be done for the strengthening of the church.[42]

Interaction refers to the process of mutual learning that took place between people during meetings. Relationships and communication were not primarily between a leader and every other member of the church, but between each and every person. Everyone had something to learn from everyone else during church get-togethers. This is indicated by the term 'one another' in the following passages:

> Speak to *one another* with psalms, hymns and spiritual songs. Sing and make music in your heart to the Lord, always giving thanks to God the Father for everything, in the name of our Lord Jesus Christ.[43]

> Let the word of Christ dwell in you richly as you teach and admonish *one another* with all wisdom, and as you

---

[42] 1 Cor 14:26 (NIV, emphasis added)
[43] Eph 5:19-20 (NIV, emphasis added)

sing psalms, hymns and spiritual songs with gratitude in your hearts to God.[44]

Let us not give up meeting together, as some are in the habit of doing, but let us encourage *one another*, and all the more as you see the Day approaching.[45]

Consequently, we can see that early church meetings were 'spiritual potlucks' in which everyone brought something that everyone else could benefit from. New Testament-style church meetings afforded each person the opportunity to make use of their spiritual gift by sharing an experience, teaching, prophecy, song, etc. There were no one-man shows, one-way communication, or formal ceremonies; rather, they were informal, spontaneous, and participatory occasions where everyone's gifts were used.

Mystical Elements: Prayer, Praise, and Singing

Prayer, praise, and singing punctuated first century gatherings and are here categorized as 'mystical' elements. The popular definitions of these three terms are that prayer is the communication of a desire to receive something from God, praise is giving to God recognition and thanks, and singing is some combination of prayer and praise set to music or expressed melodically.

Prayer, by far, was the most common form of expression to God in New Testament era churches. Believers prayed for each other, for the apostles, for those in government authority, in times of illness, during periods of persecution, when a fellow Christian was slipping into sin, for clarity during decision-making, and for a myriad of other reasons.[46] There are even several places in the scriptures where the words of a prayer are recorded.[47] Interestingly, though, in comparison to prayer (mentioned about ninety times from *Acts* to *Revelation*), there was much less said about, and few examples given of, either praise (mentioned about forty times) or singing (mentioned about a dozen times), apart from a few passing remarks. Thus, it is

---

[44] Col 3:16 (NIV, emphasis added)
[45] Heb 10:25 (NIV, emphasis added)
[46] Acts 1:24-26, 2:42, 4:24-31, 16:25; Eph 6:18-20; Philip 4:6-7; Col 4:2-4; 1 Thes 2:8, 5:17-18; 2 Thes 3:1-4; 1 Tim 2:1-4; Heb 13:18; James 5:13; 1 John 5:16; Jude 1:20
[47] Acts 1:24-25, 4:24-31 7:59-60

quite probable that this relative emphasis in the early church writings on prayer over praise and singing also characterized house church meetings.

As discussed earlier, when Christians gathered there seemed to be a great deal of spontaneity, freedom, and opportunity for *everyone* to engage in prayer (as well as praise and singing), something Paul underscored in letters to several different churches.[48] Such openness and high levels of participation would have been difficult to facilitate in a large group setting, but they were a natural outcome in the smaller more intimate context of the early house-sized churches.

Intellectual Elements: The Apostles' Teachings

Early church gatherings were also forums for the intellectual development of its members. The apostle Paul seems to have been especially keen on seeing people in his churches develop an increased understanding of the things of God with their minds. He lays such an emphasis on this throughout his letters that some might accuse the apostle of being too much of a rationalist, which may stem partially from his previous training as a Pharisee.[49] This tendency of Paul's and, presumably, of the communities he founded, is seen by the frequency of his reference to rational activity and the variety of contexts for it. He uses a significant number and variety of terms and ideas to get his point across to his audience like consider, convince, discern, grasp, instruct, judge, know, knowledge, learn, meaning, mind, persuade, reasonable, remind, teach, test, think, thoughts, truth, understanding, and wisdom.[50]

What concrete forms did this take in believers' meetings? There seemed to have been some combination of learning from those who had a clear ability to teach while at the same time honouring the principle of mutual instruction. The apostles encouraged 'teachers', those who were knowledgeable and had an obvious strength in communicating, to make use of this talent for the benefit of others.[51]

---

[48] 1 Cor 14:26, Eph 5:19-20, Col 3:16
[49] Acts 23:6, 26:5,24-25; Philip 3:4-6
[50] Acts 26:24-25; Rom 12:2, 14:5, 16:19; 1 Cor 1:10, 2:12,15, 4:6,11, 14:20,29, 15:34; 2 Cor 10:5, 11:3; Gal 3:2; Eph 4:22-24, 5:15; Philip 1:9, 2:5, 3:15, 4:8; Col 1:9-10, 3:2,10, 4:5; 1 Thes 5:21; 1 Tim 2:11, 5:4; 2 Tim 3:7; Titus 3:14; Heb 5:11-6:2
[51] Rom 12:6-7; 1 Tim 5:17; Heb 5:11

The early church believed that God had gifted certain individuals with a strong teaching ability to aid the Body of Christ.[52] Those with this capacity may have included local elders, local Christians who were not functioning as elders, and those called to travel from church to church.[53] Even so, the apostles Paul, Peter, and John all showed concern about the very real possibility that false teachers could eventually infiltrate churches and not hold true to apostolic instruction.[54] As such, all learning was to be firmly based not on people's own whims and ideas but, rather, on the teachings of the apostles—whether by word of mouth or in written form—and the scriptures.[55]

What was the format for such instruction? Was it lecture-style with one person delivering a one-way message to a crowd of quiet listeners? Quite the opposite actually. As demonstrated earlier, local churches knew they were to "teach and admonish one another with all wisdom"[56] and that "everyone has...a word of instruction"[57] during meetings. This interactive teaching method among believers was even employed by visiting apostles. A clear example of this happened when the apostle Paul visited a house church in the city of Troas:

> On the first day of the week we came together to break bread. Paul *spoke* to the people and, because he intended to leave the next day, kept on *talking* until midnight. There were many lamps in the upstairs room where we were meeting...Paul *talked* on and on... After *talking* until daylight, he left.[58]

The Greek root word used for *spoke* and *talked* in this passage is *dialegomai*, from which we get our word 'dialogue', and quite literally means to have a conversation or debate. The Greek words used for the two instances of *talking* are *logon* and *homileo*, meaning talk, converse, or reason. However, altogether different Greek words

---

[52] 1 Cor 12:28-29; Eph 4:11-12
[53] Acts 13:1, 15:36-41, 18:24-28; 1 Tim 5:17; 2 John 1:7-11
[54] 1 Tim 6:3-5; 2 Tim 4:3; Titus 1:10-11; 2 Pet 2:1-3; 2 John 1:9-11
[55] Rom 15:4; 1 Cor 15:3-5; 1 Thes 4:1-2; 2 Thes 3:14-15; 1 Tim 4:13, 5:7; 2 Tim 2:2, 3:16; 2 Pet 3:15-16
[56] Col 3:16 (NIV)
[57] 1 Cor 14:26 (NIV)
[58] Acts 20:7-12 (NIV, emphasis added)

in the New Testament are used for instances of one-way communication or 'preaching' (Greek = *kerusso* and *euangello*), which was reserved for communicating the message of Christ to non-Christians who had not heard it before.

So, Paul's teaching style was to have a lengthy two-way discussion—not a monologue—with questions and answers and more questions and ideas being formulated as the evening unfolded, albeit with Paul probably making the dominant contribution. This kind of interactive discussion and learning was the typical method employed whenever any kind of instruction was taking place in the early house churches.

Spectacular Elements: Prophecy, Tongues, and Others

A more dramatic set of occurrences was also present in early church meetings, presently classified together as 'spectacular' elements. These contributions from the different members of a local church went beyond the ordinary and humanly explainable. When these aspects presented themselves, it was clear that people were simply the vehicles and conduits for these expressions and not their originators.

Regarding the particular spectacular elements that could be present in a given meeting,[59] the list includes: prophecy (an intuitive knowledge of inner prompting to speak God's mind); tongues (speaking and interpreting a nonhuman language); healings (power over the physical effects of disease and accident); miraculous works (exorcisms of demons, nature miracles, etc.); and discernment of spirits (detecting whether a message originates with God, demons, or humans). Some explicit examples of their use during a meeting include the sensitivity of some prophets in discerning God's call on Barnabas and Paul to an apostolic ministry and the resuscitation at the hands of Paul of a young man who had fallen down dead during a late night gathering.[60]

These spiritual gifts were to be released during church meetings for the mutual benefit of all present.[61] Paul takes pains to convince

---

[59] Acts 15:32-33; 1 Cor 12:7-10, 28-30; 1 Thes 5:19-22; James 5:14-16; 1 John 4:1-3
[60] Acts 13:1-3, 20:7-12
[61] 1 Cor 14:26; 1 Thes 5:19-20

his readers to view everyone's gift as having an important role in the life of the church by comparing Christ to a head and the church to a body, the former giving direction to the latter for the benefit of every part of the body.[62] Although he argues for the uniqueness and significance of everyone's contribution, in Paul's mind some of these spectacular gifts were more inherently beneficial and intelligible to the church and curious visitors and should be strongly encouraged, especially prophesy.[63] He also emphasizes that these God-given capacities were distributed differently among people, such that not everyone would have the same type or number of these spectacular abilities.[64] Consequently, we can expect the expression of these gifts in the first century church to have varied from locality to locality and perhaps even meeting to meeting. Lastly, none of these dramatic gifts were to be suppressed, except as dictated by a sense of balance and appropriateness. Their allure seems to have been somewhat problematic for the Corinthians, forcing Paul to emphasize that things were to be done in an orderly manner so that church meetings would not become chaotic and unproductive.[65]

Symbolic Elements: The Lord's Supper and Baptism

In the early church there were two symbolic acts used to signify milestone moments in the life of Christ and, hence, in the life of the follower of Christ, namely the Lord's Supper and Baptism.

The Lord's Supper With its bread and wine, this was modeled by Christ and practiced by the ancient church around a full meal.[66] It is not entirely certain, though, whether this occurred every single time believers met together corporately—although, apparently it was a very frequent practice—or even whether more overtly 'spiritual' elements like prayer, prophecy, teaching, etc., occurred during the meal. In either case, the Lord's Supper would have evoked several key ideas and vivid images in the minds of believers. First and foremost, it was a reminder that Jesus came into the world to lay his life down willingly as a sacrifice—his broken body and spilt blood represented by the bread and wine—which somehow remedied the

---

[62] 1 Cor 12:12-27
[63] 1 Cor 14:1-6,22
[64] 1 Cor 12:4-7, 28-30
[65] 1 Cor 14:27-33,40
[66] Luke 22:14-20; 1 Cor 11:17-34

darkness and sin in the world. Being first patterned by Christ in the setting of a Passover meal, it also carried his disciples back to the story of God's rescue of the Israelite nation out of Egyptian slavery, both by instructing the angel of death to 'pass over' their homes and by leading them to 'pass over' the desert from Egypt to the Promised Land.[67] Thus, for the early church, Jesus was now rescuing them from a more sinister type of evil, that of spiritual slavery. Lastly, in the cultural framework of the first century, the fact that the Lord's Supper was indeed a full-scale community meal was a sign of mutual acceptance into an intimate and unique friendship not shared by others.[68] Those who had voluntarily forged a family bond in Christ now shared this 'community table' with each other.

Who was authorized to oversee the Lord's Supper? The scriptures are curiously silent about this issue, perhaps indicating that this was not a point of concern for the early church. The only example we have of anyone specifically administering it was Jesus himself during the last supper he shared with his twelve disciples. It would be difficult to make a case from this one-time event, though, that those in leadership always must have physically initiated the Lord's Supper during church meetings. Even so, we might reasonably infer that local leaders—being responsible for managing the overall affairs of the church—would have been at least present, although not always physically involved, during such an activity to ensure that things were done appropriately.

Baptism. This was the other major symbolic act prevalent in the early church. Christ's personal baptism at the hands of John the Baptist and his last instructions to the apostles to make and baptize disciples served as the primary model and mandate for the early Christian community.[69] Consequently, right from the birth of the church at Pentecost, new members were baptized in water as an outward sign of their inward allegiance to Christ. The baptisms recorded in the New Testament were performed both privately and publicly, in small and large groups, were reserved for believers only, and seemed to occur very soon after the first indications of genuine

---

[67] Exodus 12:1-40
[68] Mat 9:10-11, Luke 15:1-2, 1 Cor 5:9-11
[69] Mat 3:13-17, 28:18-20

faith in Christ.[70] As such, it is quite conceivable that non-Christian friends who visited a church meeting and came to faith were baptized during the meeting itself; however, no explicit report of such an event survives.

Who was qualified to administer baptism? It seemed to have been customarily done by the apostles as they gained new converts from their preaching forays, but no explicit scriptural instruction is given on this matter. We are, in fact, given some indication that perhaps any believer could legitimately baptize a new convert. For example, we are told that Philip baptized an Ethiopian man privately along the roadside as well as a large number of others.[71] Philip was not one of the twelve apostles or a recognized apostolic worker, nor was he ever referred to as an elder. Rather he was simply in charge of addressing some material needs of the Jerusalem church.[72] Similarly, John the Baptist was not commissioned by any authoritative individual or religious body to engage in his baptisms. Yet, Jesus recognized the legitimacy of the Baptist's activities not only by being baptized by him, but also by showing support for John's baptisms during a debate with the Pharisees.[73] As such, similar to the Lord's Supper, it may be that those in local leadership were present, although not always directly involved, during baptisms.

Relational Elements: 'One Another' and 'Each Other'

Jesus once made the statement that the world would know that Christians were indeed his disciples by the mutual love they demonstrated.[74] It was about building a community together, living the common life, and engaging in mutual life-on-life ministry.

---

[70] Acts 2:36-41, 8:4-17, 8:34-39, 9:17-19, 10:44-48, 16:13-15, 16:29-34, 18:7-8, 1 Cor 1:14-16; Those arguing for infant baptism find support in some instances where it is recorded that a 'household' was saved and baptized (Acts 11:11-17, 16:15, 16:31-34, 18:8; 1 Cor 1:16, 16:15), presumably including any infants. However, at best, these are arguments from silence based on vague passages, since no infants are ever mentioned explicitly on these occasions. The overwhelming scriptural evidence supports voluntary, adult, believer's baptism.

[71] Acts 8:4-13, 8:34-39

[72] Acts 6:1-6

[73] Mat 21:23-27

[74] John 13:35

The early church took this seriously enough that the writers of the New Testament made sure it was replete with dozens of 'one another' and 'each other' statements, encouraging followers of Christ to consider the many ways they could practically and mutually show love. Although not elements solely restricted to church meetings, the force behind their sentiment was certainly felt during house church get-togethers and would have been a distinguishing hallmark immediately noted by the observant visitor. The 'one another' and 'each other' passages touch on themes of mutual acceptance, admonition, agreement, building up, compassion, concern, confession, devotion, encouragement, fellowship, forgiveness, greeting, harmony, honour, hospitality, humility, instruction, kindness, love, peaceability, prayer, service, submission, and tolerance.[75]

The apostles also gave directives concerning things *not* to do to 'one another' and 'each other' such as deceiving, envying, grumbling against, judging, provoking, and slandering.[76] These items were not meant merely to be part of a litany of ideals to be aspired to and discussed theoretically but, rather, were to characterize interactions between believers on a day-to-day level.

The apostles were certainly keenly aware of the practical need for such constant reminders because New Testament home churches were by nature small and intimate clusters of people and, as such, held great potential for tension and division. Conversely, the apostles knew that forging deep, authentic, and mutually transforming friendships could only occur in such intimate gatherings. This may have been another reason why their practice was to pattern the early Christian communities using a house church model.

Evangelistic Elements: When Non-Christians Visit

As described above, most of the evangelistic activities of the first Christians were customarily done out in the public eye, whereas private house-to-house patterns were reserved for believers. Evangelism, however, was not strictly limited to the public forum, but also wove its way into the house churches whenever curious

---

[75] Rom 12:10, 12:16, 15:7, 15:14, 16:16; 1 Cor 1:10, 12:25, 16:20; 2 Cor 13:12; Gal 5:13; Eph 4:2, 4:32, 5:21; Philip 4:2; Col 3:13, 3:16; 1 Thes 3:12, 4:9,18, 5:11,13,15,25; 2 Thes 1:3; Heb 3:13, 10:24, 13:1; James 4:11, 5:16; 1 Pet 1:22, 3:8, 4:7-11, 5:5,14; 1 John 1:7, 3:11,23, 4:7,12; 2 John 1:5
[76] Gal 5:26; Col 3:9; James 4:11, 5:9

friends and neighbours visited. In giving the Corinthian Christians instructions about church gatherings, Paul encourages them to be aware of the opportunity that exists to intelligently communicate the message of Christ when visitors come.[77] Specifically, he counsels them to avoid the use of the gift of tongues—usually unintelligible unless there is someone who can interpret the message—in favour of prophecy as a more meaningful tool in this regard, convincing the seeker to surrender their lives to Christ. That such things actually took place from time to time may be inferred from the very fact that Paul brings the issue to light. Evidently, when this occurred it must have been a profoundly moving experience for all involved as the visitor encounters God for the first time before everyone's eyes.

Although not a church gathering as such, another similar example, spelled out in some detail, is that of the apostle Peter visiting the home of Cornelius, the Roman officer whose prayers God had heard.[78] Cornelius, being a man of some position and local influence, invited a house full of friends in anticipation of the apostle's visit. Before Peter even came to the end of his message, the Holy Spirit fell on the hearers, and they began speaking in tongues and praising God. After this, they were all baptized in water. Peter stayed on for a few days, at the new house church's request, instructing them as to what the next steps were to be. Because Cornelius' relational circle experienced such a dramatic encounter with God, it is probable that they became particularly keen on the need to invite others from their family and social networks into future house gatherings, hoping to see other conversions take place.

Material Elements: Sharing the Wealth

As in any era, the New Testament Christians were faced with the challenges of dealing deftly with material needs and financial decisions. The general principle endorsed by Christ and the apostles was that of a lifestyle of generosity that gave of itself, not under compulsion, but voluntarily and gladly.[79] What did early believers focus their financial generosity on? Certainly, as a house church movement, it would not have been on any church buildings or expensive programs. The early church gave money almost exclu-

---

[77] 1 Cor 14:22-25
[78] Acts 10:1-48
[79] Mark 12:41-44; 2 Cor 9:6-8

sively to two groups of people, namely the poor among them and traveling apostolic workers. However, the financial support of traveling leaders, and their local counterparts, is discussed later under the category of New Testament era leadership. So, the current brief discussion will be limited to the church's efforts to address the twin problems of local and universal poverty issues.

Local Needs. Local poverty relief was something close to the heart of first century believers, since many of them were faced with very real material needs of their own. In the early days after Pentecost, the Jerusalem church was faced with the problem of addressing the needs of the burgeoning Christian community, now suddenly numbering over 3,000 members. This mass of people was from all over the Mediterranean world and had decided to settle in Jerusalem to be with their new spiritual family. The apostles now had an emergency on their hands and had to deal with the consequences of their successful preaching. It is reported that the solution to the situation was a pooling of everyone's resources into a common pot— possibly collected by both the traveling apostles and local leaders— which was drawn upon to meet whatever material needs anyone had. It seemed to work well.[80] Additionally, some churches evidently had local widows, without any surviving family, who were being taken care of by their Christian community.[81]

Universal Needs. Local believers, however, were not only concerned with their own situation, but they took notice of the plight of their brothers and sisters in other parts of the world. For example, years after Pentecost the situation for the Jerusalem church did not see much improvement, this time due to a famine as was known to happen in that part of the world from time to time. Consequently, the apostles Peter, James, and John made an arrangement with the apostles Paul and Barnabas to undertake a fundraising project among some of his Gentile churches to relieve the suffering of the church in Jerusalem. Paul went on to specifically request that the Corinthians and Galatians set aside weekly amounts, depending on their own financial situation, on a regular basis until he came so that no collections would have to be made at the last moment. We are told it was the local house church elders who accepted contributions every

---

[80] Acts 2:43-45, 4:32-35
[81] 1 Tim 5:3,9,16

week at the house church meetings, passing the sum to Paul and Barnabas when they came to collect.[82]

Temporal Elements: Day, Time, and Length of Meetings

Another topic of interest is the temporal characteristics of the early Christian communities. In other words, what habits did they have when it came to choosing the day, time, and length of their gatherings?

Regarding the choice of day and time, there seems to have been in some cases a preference to meet on the first day of the week, i.e. Sunday, to commemorate the resurrection of the Christ by breaking bread together.[83] Paul, however, took pains to ensure that communities he was connected with were not becoming too rigidly attached to any particular day of the week as being more sacred than any other.[84] Accordingly, it is reported that the early church felt free to meet on any day of the week, morning and evening, as circumstances dictated.[85]

Regarding the length of time for a given church meeting, there was no clear apostolic practice. Meetings could be open ended and very long, as was the case when Paul visited a house church for an all night discussion session that lasted until daybreak.[86] Similarly, when Herod arrested the apostle Peter, believers in Jerusalem met with their respective home churches and spent all night praying for his release.[87] The general rule for meeting duration seems to have been the particular need of the moment.

Sociological Elements: The Size of House Churches

From personal experience and sociological research, we know that the size of any group will affect the individual relationships between members, overall group dynamics, and the learning process.[88]

---

[82] Acts 11:27-30, Rom 15:25-28, 1 Cor 16:1-4, 2 Cor 9:1-15, Gal 2:1,9-10
[83] Luke 24:1-7; Acts 20:7-11; 1 Cor 16:2
[84] Rom 14:4-6, Gal 4:8-11, Col 2:16-17
[85] Acts 1:12-14, 2:46-47, 5:42, 6:1, 16:5; Heb 3:13
[86] Acts 20:7-11
[87] Acts 12:11-17
[88] Susan Imel, "Using Groups in Adult Learning: Theory and Practices", *The Journal of Continuing Education in the Health Professions*, Vol. 19, 1999, pp.54-61; Levine, J.M. and R.L. Moreland, "Small Groups", in

Consequently, another important matter to understand is the sociological factor of group size in first-century churches.

Let us first consider whether we have any record of how many people were involved in a typical first-century house church. Unfortunately, we have few direct statements in the New Testament about the size of the average local gathering of believers and certainly no apostolic directives. There are, however, a few clues that are worth teasing out.

The small band of twelve disciples gathered around Jesus may serve as a model in this regard.[89] Although not technically a house church after the manner of the Pauline churches, Christ's discipleship circle would have at least implicitly and naturally served as a prototype for the faith communities that the apostles founded. As a small group, Christ and his disciples gathered together in a home with a 'large upper room' to celebrate the Passover together.[90] This intimate setting was ideal for the type of intense interaction they apparently had, which involved foot washing, sharing a meal, taking part in the Lord's Supper in anticipation of Jesus' impending arrest and death, hymn singing, and heart rending conversations about denial and betrayal.[91]

Another clue as to the size of a typical Christian cluster is found in the account relating events just prior to Pentecost.[92] The group included between twelve and perhaps one hundred and twenty disciples at any one time in the upper room of a Jerusalem home, where they were continually wrestling in prayer together.

A further insight comes from Peter's visit to the home of Cornelius the Roman officer. We are told that there was a large gathering of people assembled to hear the message Peter was about to bring.[93] Since the listeners all became followers of Christ that day, we can probably assume that this 'large gathering' continued to meet together as a newly formed house church.

Gilbert, Fiske, Lindzey, eds., *The Handbook of Social Psychology*, 4th edition, Boston: McGraw-Hill, 1998, pp.415-469.
[89] Mark 3:13-19
[90] Mark 14:13-15
[91] Mark 14:17-26, John 13:1-38
[92] Acts 1:13-15
[93] Acts 10:19-27

Although the scriptural information we have is rather scanty there is, fortunately, archaeological evidence that indicates the physical size of the average home. First century houses were able to accommodate at most thirty or thiry-five individuals comfortably.[94] Thus, a large church would have been one that was filled to the brim with perhaps as many as three-dozen people. Many house churches were probably significantly smaller than this and, hence, were more reminiscent of Jesus' first discipleship circle of twelve. Either way, the small group dynamic helped maintain a kind of up-close-and-personal family atmosphere in house churches, where everyone knew each other and had the opportunity to interact on a more intimate level. Consequently, apostolic directives to the churches—interactive meetings, mutual accountability, the Lord's Supper as a full meal, relationships, etc.—make much practical sense with this understanding in mind.

4. WHAT ABOUT LEADERSHIP IN THE EARLY CHURCH?

The New Testament presents a clear role for human leadership. To drive the movement, the early church primarily utilized two types of leaders, namely local leaders and mobile leaders.[95]

Local Leaders

Description. Local leaders were natives of an area who had been appointed by traveling apostolic workers to take on the responsibilities of the church in their immediate vicinity. Ideally, the practice was to have two types of local labourers, namely 'presbyters' (Greek = *presbuteros*, meaning 'elder') and 'deacons' (Greek = *diakonos*, meaning 'servant' or 'minister'). It is important to note that the term 'bishop' (Greek = *episkopos*, meaning 'overseer'), which appears several times, is interchangeable with 'elder/presbyter'. They mean the same thing. This can be seen from a cross comparison of key scriptures.[96] Any distinction between them in our minds is merely artificial and based on historical developments rather than biblical warrant. Thus, locally there were two types of leaders involved, elders and deacons.

---

[94] Del Birkey, *The House Church*, Scottdale: Herald Press, 1988, p.55.
[95] see *Appendix 2 – The Early Church as an Organized Movement*
[96] Acts 20:17,28-30; 1 Tim 3:1-13; Titus 1:5-9; 1 Pet 5:1-3

Function. The role of elders was local and ongoing. They were the primary spiritual nurturers, teachers, and coaches of a local community of believers. When someone was sick, they were called in to pray.[97] When someone needed clarification on a scriptural matter, they were involved.[98] When major decisions affecting the strategic direction of the church were made, they were key people in the process.[99] Deacons seemed to have assisted the elders in managing the affairs of the church, particularly when it came to finances and material needs.[100] Both these led the church as parents would lead a family, not in a dictatorial manner but through their humble and loving attitude and hard work.[101] The writer of Hebrews encouraged Christians to 'obey' (Greek = *peitho*, meaning to 'be persuaded or convinced by') and 'submit' (Greek = *hupeiko*, meaning to 'yield or give in') to their leaders.[102] However, this did not mean a blind and unthinking submission to leadership, but rather a willingness to go along with leaders when there was an impasse. The authority of elders and deacons was held in check by the involvement of the entire body at various decision-making moments.[103]

Organization. Paul was concerned to see elders appointed in each 'church' and 'town'.[104] There initially seems to be some confusion about the exact distribution of elders because of the multipurpose use of the term 'church', which could refer to a single home church,[105] a citywide church,[106] or a regional church.[107] However, evidence suggests that in the first-century Jewish synagogue system—which provided the cultural and religious background for the emergence of the early Christian house churches—a team of elders was responsible for each local syna-

---

[97] James 5:14
[98] Titus 1:9-11
[99] Acts 15:2-6,22
[100] Acts 6:1-6
[101] Mat 20:25-28; 1 Thes 5:12-13; 1 Pet 5:3; Heb 13:7
[102] Heb 13:17
[103] Mat 18:15-17; Acts 6:1-6, 15:22
[104] Acts 14:23; Titus 1:5
[105] Rom 16:1-5; 1 Cor 16:19
[106] Acts 8:1, 11:26; 1 Cor 1:2; 2 Cor 1:1; 1 Thes 1:1; 2 Thes 1:1
[107] Acts 9:31

gogue.[108] Similarly, the biblical record lends itself to a plurality of elders[109] managing a given Christian community, rather than any one individual. Thus, ideally, each house church would likely have had a small group of elders, if such qualified individuals were available. They, in turn, were part of a larger citywide or regional team that managed their network of home churches. Deacons, on the other hand, were perhaps only supplemental roles that were filled depending on the need. This can be inferred from Paul and Timothy's discussions regarding both elders and deacons in Ephesus and Philippi, while only elders are mentioned as the apostle Titus nurtured the churches of Crete.[110]

Qualifications. In writing to his fellow apostolic workers Timothy and Titus, Paul provides guidelines regarding the qualifications of elders and deacons.[111] He specifies two broad categories, namely moral integrity and basic management skills, for both elders and deacons. Paul, though, adds the ability to teach as necessary for an elder. He recognized that if a local worker was weak in any one of these areas or was a recent convert, it could hinder the spiritual growth of Christians and potentially be an obstacle for non-Christians to becoming followers of Christ. Both character and competence had to be evident in someone who aspired to lead the church locally.

Training. Although there is no direct evidence concerning the exact way local leaders were developed, several patterns emerge. First, *apostolic coaching* was directly involved in the training and selection of local leaders. This was especially the case when a new church was started as the first generation of leaders emerged. On five separate occasions, Paul stayed locally for 1½ to 3 years to ensure that local churches were healthy and strong, including the proper training of elders.[112] Paul would sometimes gather local leaders

---

[108] Richard Ascough, *What are they saying about the Formation of Pauline Churches?* Mahwah, New Jersey: Paulist Press, 1998, p.13; see also Mark 5:22, Luke 7:1-5, and Acts 13:15 which indicate plural leadership in each local synagogue
[109] Acts 11:30, 14:23, 15:2-6,22, 16:4, 20:17, 21:18; 1 Tim 4:14, 5:17; James 5:14; 1 Pet 5:1
[110] Philip 1:1; 1 Tim 3:1,8; Titus 1:5
[111] 1 Tim 3:1-13; Titus 1:5-9
[112] Acts 18:11, 19:10, 20:31, 24:27, 28:30

together for a private meeting apart from the rest of the church to discuss leadership issues.[113] In other situations Paul, as the more experienced apostle, gave the responsibility of appointing elders and deacons to younger apostles like Timothy and Titus.[114]

Second, a *discipleship chain* mentality was evident. Paul saw his job not simply as gaining many followers and doing the work himself, but in making capable leaders of younger apostles (Timothy), the local leaders they trained ('faithful men'), and the next generation ('others also').[115] It is significant to notice that Paul's practice was to have direct apostolic involvement in a church only temporarily until it was well established; subsequent generations of leaders were to be trained and appointed locally.

Third, an *apprenticeship model* was employed, ensuring up-close-and-personal training. Preparation of local leaders would have consisted of practical on-the-job experiences as they laboured side-by-side with and learned from the example of apostolic workers.[116]

Accountability. If an elder was getting seriously off track, it was the responsibility of an apostolic worker in relationship with that church or another local elder to address the problem. But this step was only to be taken after the evidence of two or three witnesses was brought to bear.[117] In a well-known case, a local elder named Diotrephes attempted to gain personal prominence and power and was unwilling to work with traveling Christian workers.[118] After several people verified the complaint, the apostle John—also a local elder himself—made plans for a personal visit to deal with the situation.

Financial Support. What about the monetary support of local leaders in the early church? There is one passage in the New Testament, in particular, which is often put forward as an example of the existence of salaried local elders in the first century. In writing to his co-apostle Timothy about the elders in the city of Ephesus, Paul states that they should receive "double honor" for their labours since,

---

[113] Acts 20:17
[114] 1 Tim 3:1-13; 2 Tim 2:2; Titus 1:5-9
[115] 2 Tim 2:2
[116] 1 Thes 2:5-10
[117] 1 Tim 5:19
[118] 3 John

by analogy, an ox should not be muzzled while it is treading out grain and workers deserve their wages.[119] However, there are four reasons why this probably does not refer to a regular salary.

First, the actual word used in the passage for "honor" (Greek = *time*) is also used over forty times in other places in the New Testament, having the force of respect or value, but not finances as such. There is another perfectly good Greek word for pay, wages, or salary (Greek = *misthos*) that is used thirty-eight times in the New Testament which, significantly, is not present in the phrase "double honor".

Second, while visiting these same local elders in Ephesus on another occasion, Paul encouraged them to follow his example by working hard with their own hands to meet their material needs and those of others.[120] It would certainly be a notable inconsistency if Paul were to encourage full-time salaries for elders on one occasion and then on another to actually discourage it.

Third, in the first century Jewish synagogue system—as a precursor to the early Christian house churches—the team of elders that managed the spiritual affairs of the Jewish community did so on a strictly voluntary basis.[121] This influence certainly would not have been lost on Paul in organizing house churches.

Fourth, there would not necessarily have been any practical reason for the early house churches to ever employ local elders. A small team of three or four volunteer elders could have easily facilitated a New Testament style house church—which had no more than thirty members—without requiring financial support from that community.

Thus, the weight of the evidence is that the phrase "double honor" refers not to financial support at all, but rather to the rightful rewards of an elder being the increased respect, appreciation, and admiration he rightfully gains from the people he serves and leads.[122] Certainly, if an elder suddenly faced a personal financial crisis or if

---

[119] 1 Tim 5:17-18
[120] Acts 20:33-35
[121] R.C.H. Lenski, *The Interpretation of St. Paul's Epistles to the Thessalonians, to Titus, and to Philemon*, Columbus, Ohio: Wartburg Press, 1946, p.683.
[122] A good parallel passage is 1 Thes 5:12-13.

the house church wanted to give an occasional gift to them, they certainly would have been free to do so.[123] Thus, local house church elders were volunteers who had jobs like everyone else in the church.

Mobile Leaders

Description. The early church also had a select group who were mobile workers traveling from place to place to strengthen and grow the churches. The primary type of traveling labourer in the first century was the 'apostle' (Greek = *apostolos*, meaning 'sent one', 'envoy', 'ambassador', or 'messenger').

Function. Unlike the function of elders and deacons, which was long term and localized, the job description of these apostles was temporary and universal. They were builders who laid the spiritual foundations in a new city or region. Apostles, in essence, established new self-sustaining disciplemaking communities in unreached areas and provided future coaching when necessary. They would preach the message, gather their converts into homes, and appoint qualified locals to lead the church after they departed. They also returned from time to time to invigorate and instruct, flowing from church to church. It is significant that Paul stayed for up to several years on five occasions,[124] spending only weeks or months on other occasions when circumstances became personally dangerous.[125] The scriptures record at least fifteen individuals who lived this nomadic apostolic life—at least for a season—and could be called Paul-type apostles.[126]

There were also James-type apostles, though, who did not seem to travel as extensively, but rather had a wider geographic region or population demographic for which they were responsible. Examples of these include James[127] (who seemed to have remained in Jerusalem), John[128] (who may have cared for a regional network of churches), and at times Peter[129] (who directed the affairs of the church in Jerusalem just after Pentecost and/or occasionally would

---

[123] Gal 6:6
[124] Acts 18:11, 19:10, 20:31, 24:27, 28:30
[125] Acts 16:12, 18:23, 19:8, 20:6, 21:4, 21:27
[126] Acts 15:30-16:12, 20:1-5; 1 Cor 4:14-17; Philip 2:25, 4:3; 1 Thes 1:1; 2 Tim 4:10
[127] Acts 21:17-18, Gal 1:18-19, 2:9-12
[128] 3 John; Rev 1:9-11
[129] Acts 8:14-25; Acts 11:19-23; Gal 2:1,9

visit to strengthen an existing or new body of believers). Understandably then, they sometimes had the double duty of being mobile apostles and local elders and referred to themselves as such.[130]

Organization. In contrast to the shared leadership of local elders, apostolic teams seemed to have one or two senior members who had a slightly greater level of influence. For example, among the twelve apostles chosen by Jesus, after his resurrection Christ passed on the baton of leadership to Peter in particular.[131] None of the remaining twelve had such an interaction with Christ. A few weeks later, during the early days after Pentecost, Peter acted as the primary spokesman, authority figure, and initiative taker in the Jerusalem church.[132] Similarly, although Paul almost always worked as past of a team of apostolic workers, he seemed to have been the senior member of the group. His was the name that appeared first in all the letters sent to churches by him and his cohorts.[133] He also directed the comings, goings, and activities of his junior co-workers.[134] Although there were other Christians working in the Gentile world, the twelve apostles back in Jerusalem recognized Paul as the chief apostle to the Gentiles.[135] The reason for this apparent concentration of leadership in one or two individuals is that apostolic bands were not churches in the same sense that local 'ekklesias' were, but they were teams on a very specific mission. Although it can safely be assumed that there was 'churching' going on between members of these groups, that was not their main purpose; hence, leadership was not necessarily structured the same way as it was locally.

Qualifications. Who could rightfully claim to be an apostle in the early church? Qualified individuals were recognized in two ways. Primary-type apostles were those personally chosen, trained, and/or sent by Jesus Christ himself and would have also had a personal visit from Christ after his resurrection. They were the spiritual heavy weights that were the norm for doctrine and practice in the early

---

[130] 1 Pet 1:1, 5:1; 2 and 3 John 1:1
[131] John 21:15-17
[132] Acts 2:14,37-40; Acts 4:8, 5:3, 9:32, 10
[133] 1 Cor 1:1; 2 Cor 1:1; Gal 1:1-2; Philip 1:1; Col 1:1; 1 and 2 Thes 1:1
[134] Acts 16:9-10, 17:15, 19:22; Eph 6:22; Philip 2:19; Col 4:7-8; 1 and 2 Tim; Titus
[135] Gal 2:7-9

church, having authored or given approval to all the books in the New Testament. This unique and one-time-only list included the original Twelve, James the Lord's brother, Paul, and a number of others.[136] Secondary-type apostles were those chosen, trained, and/or sent by the church, but who did not necessarily have a post-resurrection encounter with Christ. They were trained by and merely repeated what the Primary-type apostles did in carrying out their own mandate, and included the likes of Apollos, Barnabas, Luke, Silas, Timothy, Titus, etc.[137] Although having a spotless moral reputation was never adequate qualification by itself to be an apostle, it certainly was present and necessary.[138]

Training. Christ was a traveling kingdom worker who helped train the first generation of 'sent ones' by using training techniques similar to that for local elders discussed earlier. He used the principles of personal coaching, discipleship chains, and apprentice-ship. However, unlike the education of local leaders, the training of apostolic workers is vividly detailed in scripture. It is reported that Jesus sent out a group of his apostles-to-be to travel and preach from village to village. He gave detailed directives for this practical hands-on assignment:

> After this the Lord appointed seventy-two others and sent them two by two ahead of him to every town and place where he was about to go. He told them, "The harvest is plentiful, but the workers are few. Ask the Lord of the harvest, therefore, to send out workers into his harvest field. Go! I am sending you out like lambs among wolves. Do not take a purse or bag or sandals; and do not greet anyone on the road. When you enter a house, first say, 'Peace to this house.' If a man of peace is there, your peace will rest on him; if not, it will return to you. Stay in that house, eating and drinking whatever they give you, for the worker deserves his wages. Do not move around from house to house. When you enter a town and are wel-

---

[136] Mark 3:13-19; Luke 6:13; Acts 1:21-22; Rom 16:7; 1 Cor 9:1, 15:3-9; Gal 1:18-19
[137] Acts 13:1-3; Acts 14:3,14,20,23; Acts 20:4-5; Rom 16:21; 1 Cor 3:22; 2 Cor 8:23; Philip 1:1, 4:3; 1 Tim 4:14
[138] Acts 11:22-24; 1 Thes 2:5-12; 2 Tim 3:10-11

comed, eat what is set before you. Heal the sick who are there and tell them, 'The kingdom of God is near you.' But when you enter a town and are not welcomed, go into its streets and say, 'Even the dust of your town that sticks to our feet we wipe off against you. Yet be sure of this: The kingdom of God is near.'"[139]

Several interesting strands emerge from this example. First, Jesus organized his trainees into small teams, most likely for the sake of mutual accountability and support. Second, they were to rely on God to meet their physical needs while they stayed focused on the task of looking for a house of peace. Third, if they found such a person, they were to enjoy the hospitality of their host and see this as God's provision for them. Fourth, they were to stay in that home and build a base of operations there. This 'house of peace' would act as the spiritual outpost within that particular town or village. Fifth, Jesus and his disciples were mobile workers, whose job it was to start house churches that remained local within a given community. Sixth, they never spent an undue amount of time in a given community that resisted their message, but moved on in search of a more receptive audience. Both Peter and Paul copied this simple yet powerful approach modeled by Christ himself in their personal apostolic mandates and in training other mobile labourers.[140]

Accountability. Apostolic workers were accountable to other apostles and even local elders. For example, three years after Paul began his apostolic mission, he made an initial fifteen-day visit to some of the apostles.[141] Years later when he wanted confirmation of his message and methodology for fear of having carried out his mission in vain, Paul again privately visited the apostles and elders in Jerusalem.[142] In another situation, apostles went head-to-head publicly, Paul confronting Peter about being double-minded when it came to recognizing non-Jewish converts as legitimate Christians.[143] What the outcome of that conversation was is not specified. In the

---

[139] Luke 10:1-11 (NIV)
[140] Acts 10:1-48, 16:9-15, 20:4; 2 Tim 2:2, 3:10-11; Titus 1:5
[141] Gal 1:17-20
[142] Acts 15:1-6 cf. Gal 1:18-19; Gal 2:1-10
[143] Gal 2:11-21

case of the similar Paul-and-Barnabas face-off, this time over methodology, these two apostles parted ways.[144]

Financial Support. The support of traveling apostolic leaders was a funding focus of the early church, in addition to addressing local and universal poverty issues. The first example is that of Jesus himself, who was functionally a mobile kingdom worker for about three years. Christ was supported by a group of women who followed him around with the express intention of caring for his material needs, while it was Judas who probably managed their donations since he was the group's treasurer.[145] Other sources of assistance came in the form of the frequent offers of hospitality[146] he accepted as he traveled about the Palestinian countryside preaching, teaching, and healing.

In a similar fashion, Jesus trained his disciples to become apostolic workers by sending seventy of them out in pairs to preach from town to town as a practical hands-on exercise. They were instructed to accept the hospitality of anyone who offered it and who was open to their message of the kingdom.[147] Once the church got off the ground at Pentecost, the apostles would look to the example of Jesus in garnering support for their own itinerant responsibilities. Most of the apostles—like Peter, Jesus' brothers, and others—did accept such material assistance as they traveled. However, Paul and Barnabas, although recognizing it was their right to expect it, were most often content working for a living to meet their own needs and those of their traveling companions. Their motivation seems to have been to avert any accusations from rivals or enemies that they were in it for the money, although on occasion they gratefully accepted such support from churches that really wanted to help them out.[148]

Lastly, it is probable that support for apostolic workers was collected beforehand by local house church elders for a planned visit, given spontaneously when their visit to a house church was brief or unannounced, and regularly on an ongoing basis for apostolic workers who had to remain local for some time to set things in order.

---

[144] Acts 15:36-41
[145] Mat 27:55-56; John 12:4-6, 13:29
[146] Mat 8:14-15, 9:9-10; Luke 7:36, 10:38-42, 19:2-6
[147] Luke 10:1-11
[148] Acts 20:33-34, 1 Cor 9:1-18, Philip 4:14-19

5. HOW WAS THE EARLY CHURCH CONNECTED AS A MOVEMENT?

Was the early church a scattered bunch of house groups peppered across the vastness of the Roman Empire, going it alone? Or, was there a kind of glue that bound them together to guarantee doctrinal accuracy, sustainable growth, and clear vision? Biblically, the theology promoted by the apostles that the church is united, that the body of Christ is one, was played out in their efforts to connect— relationally if not organizationally—into a cohesive body. Sociologically, the idea and reality of belonging to an expanding global movement certainly added a sense of being part of something bigger than just one's own house church and gave people a bigger vision for what God was doing in the world at large and what their role in that was. As such, there seem to have been several key components working simultaneously toward this end, namely traveling workers, house-to-house patterns, and citywide gatherings.[149]

Traveling Apostolic Workers

The itinerant apostolic workers in the early church who had the responsibility of coaching the growing house church movement did so primarily in two ways, namely personal visits and letters. The purpose of both was the instruction, correction, and encouragement of believers as well as for preaching and healing engagements in public places to reach not-yet-Christians. They were, in effect, circuit riders.

Apostolic Visits. Personal visits to churches were a common feature of apostolic activity. A well-known example is that of Paul and Barnabas, who undertook a journey to personally deliver an important letter from Jerusalem back to their home in Antioch.[150] After they completed their mission, they set out to visit every city where they had preached in order to strengthen the churches there.[151] What they did in each city is uncertain, although some clues are given during Paul's visit to the church of Ephesus. Once there, he called the elders of the citywide church together and reminded them

---

[149] also see *Appendix 2 – The Early Church as an Organized Movement*
[150] Acts 15:23-29
[151] Acts 15:36-41

of how he taught them "publicly and from house to house",[152] indicating both a citywide and circulating house church pattern employed by the apostle.

Others involved in this kind of work included Peter, John, Apollos, and a number of Paul's traveling companions.[153] For those engaged in this kind of mobile ministry, there was a great deal of personal risk because of the physical dangers of traveling widely in the first century as well as the high financial cost and effort to do so.[154] That they did so at all is a testament to both their courage and conviction that God was calling them to give their lives for the body of Christ and see the Jesus movement continually expand.

Apostolic Letters. To supplement personal visits, there was also ongoing communication through letters, fully half of the New Testament being written to local Christian groups. In one instance, Paul specifically instructs his readers to circulate his letter to Christians in a neighbouring city and that they make certain to obtain their own copy of the letter he wrote to these neighbours.[155] On other occasions, there is strong encouragement by apostolic workers and overseers to the churches to value their written communications as authoritatively as their personal visits.[156] Although less physically risky for the writers, there was a different kind of danger—more insidious and subtle—that accompanied this kind of work, that of deceit. There was an apparent attempt by some individual or groups to actually forge a letter using the apostle Paul's name in order to promote their particular pet teaching to one group of Christians.[157]

House-to-House Patterns

Although not described in detail, there is some indication from the biblical account that some sort of face-to-face contact between individual house churches existed in a given city or region. A glimpse is given to the reader of such a house-to-house pattern actually functioning in Jerusalem. Shortly after Pentecost, the Jerusalem church found itself numbering in the thousands. They

---

[152] Acts 20:20
[153] Acts 8:14-25, 10:1-48, 18:24-27, 20:4-6; 1 Cor 9:5; 1 Pet 5:1
[154] 2 Cor 11:26-28
[155] Col 4:16
[156] 2 Thes 2:15, 3:14
[157] 2 Thes 2:2

apparently "broke bread in their homes and ate together" and met "from house to house", which would be a natural thing to do for those seeking to live a shared life together.[158] These phrases may suggest some combination of one house group visiting another house group, numerous members of a house church taking turns to open up their homes for gatherings, and/or individuals participating in more than one home gathering. The details of how this would have taken place are unclear and were probably determined based on the situation in the absence of any apostolic instruction. That this house-to-house pattern was organized or scheduled on a rotating basis is possible, although there is no hard evidence for it from the scriptures.

Citywide Gatherings

The record shows that all individual believers and house churches considered themselves as part of a single citywide church. As such, for both Jewish and Gentile Christians, citywide gatherings were employed as part of the experience of being a Christian and as an expression of unity with other believers.

Jewish Christians frequented the Temple courts in Jerusalem, sometimes *en masse*, prior to its destruction in A.D. 70, as a supplement to meeting in homes.[159] So, in Jerusalem at least, for a temporary transitional period of time, the church employed both small group believers' meetings and large group events. Large group citywide gatherings also happened when there was a controversial topic that needed to be discussed. For example, Jerusalem believers met over the controversial topic of what to do with non-Jews who were becoming Christians. Should they be required to uphold Jewish religious customs because of the Judaic roots of Christian faith, or were they free of that obligation? This was an issue, we are told, which engaged the apostles, the elders, and, to some degree, the whole church in the process.[160]

What did the Gentile churches outside Judea do to supplement their home gatherings? It is reasonable to assume that in a given town, given their sense of connectedness to one another and the fact that Paul addressed all believers in a city or region as a single church

---

[158] Acts 2:46, 5:42 (NIV)
[159] Acts 2:46, 5:42
[160] Acts 15:22

body,[161] they may have all gathered together as a larger body from time to time in some open field, on a hillside, or in a rented space, for a specific decision-making purpose. Additionally, when an apostle like Paul visited, he would apparently stop by each house church personally and also gather all the house church elders in that city together for some sort of public endeavor, either for an evangelistic purpose or for training.[162] Mass get-togethers seemed to be an occasional and special event rather than a frequent and ongoing feature of daily church life; they were no competition to the dominant practice of home meetings.

6. HOW DID THE EARLY CHURCH GROW?

People came to know Christ through a variety of methods used by the first Christians. The four primary approaches were public proclamation, private conversation, power encounters, and proliferation of new house churches. A study of the New Testament reveals that these were not expensive and highly organized programs or projects dependent on mere human genius, but rather natural, spontaneous, passionate, prayer empowered, and Spirit-led expressions of faith.[163] Thus, the general principle of first-century outreach can best be described as wherever, whenever, whoever, and however.

Public Proclamation

A very common apostolic practice was that of verbal proclamation of the message of Christ in a public setting. The strategy used by the apostles was to find an area in a town that acted as a natural gathering place for its citizens, whether it was a riverbank, a synagogue, the Jerusalem Temple courts, a lecture hall, or a marketplace. They would then verbally present the good news of Christ. Typically, they would tailor their message to suit their hearers, thereby making it seem less foreign. Paul, for example, appealed to his well-educated Greek listeners by weaving into his talk references to Greek religion and poetry as a connection point.[164] Similarly, when talking with a Jewish audience, apostles and evangelists would relate how Christ was the fulfillment of many Old

---

[161] Rom 1:7; 1 Cor 1:2; Gal 1:1; Eph 1:1; Philip 1:1
[162] Acts 20:17-21
[163] Acts 1:8, 2:1-4, 4:31,33, 8:14, 8:26-40, 10-11, 13:1-4, 16:6-10
[164] Acts 17:16-28

Testament prophecies and was, in fact, the long-awaited Jewish Messiah.[165] In both situations, anyone who responded positively to the message of Christ would either be encouraged to join an existing home church or, if this was a new work in the area, would be encouraged to open up their own home as the first spiritual beach head in that town. This approach in looking for a 'man of peace' was modeled by Jesus and imitated by both Peter and Paul.[166]

Private Conversation

Individual believers also had private conversations with and prayed for people in need on an individual basis. These were not programmed or planned endeavors, but rather spontaneous interactions during the daily ebb-and-flow of life, sometimes referred to as 'lifestyle evangelism'. Whether they were walking by the roadside (Philip and the Ethiopian eunuch), languishing in jail (Paul and the Philippian jailer), visiting someone's home (Peter and Cornelius; Ananias and Saul), or when a non-believer visited a home meeting, ancient Christians were always awake to the opportunities of sharing Christ with others in a natural unforced conversational way.[167]

Power Encounters

A common feature accompanying both public proclamation and private evangelistic conversation was supernatural healing and exorcism, sometimes referred to today as 'power encounters'. There are several stirring New Testament reports of large groups responding positively to the message brought by Christians because of the miracles that were done by God through their hands.[168] In a typical episode, so much healing and demonic deliverance was wrought through the apostles' hands in Jerusalem that large crowds were even gathering from neighbouring cities. Some were laying their sick on the ground in the streets hoping that Peter's shadow would pass over them and heal them. Consequently, there was a steady stream of people continually added to the church.[169]

---

[165] Acts 2:14-40, 7:1-54, 9:16-42, 17:2-3
[166] Luke 9:1-6, 10:1-11; Acts 2:1-3:26, 5:12-14, 6:9, 8:5-8, 9:20, 13:14-16, 14:1-7, 16:13-18, 17:1-5,17, 18:4,24-28, 19:8-10
[167] Acts 8:26-39, 9:1-20, 10:1-48, 16:25-34; 1 Cor 14:24-25; 1 Pet 3:15
[168] Acts 3:1-4:4, 8:5-13, 19:11-12, 28:1-10
[169] Acts 5:12-16

Planting and Multiplying New House Churches

Lastly, although never stated explicitly, whenever a house church grew to exceed the physical limitations of the host home, it is safe to conclude that Christians would simply multiply the group into two or send a few people out to start a new home church. This is the most probable scenario because the first-century church never owned any property or constructed any buildings. This can be inferred from the fact that a given town or city (e.g. Jerusalem, Ephesus, and Rome) contained numerous homes that hosted Christian meetings.[170]

7. DID THE APOSTLES EXPECT CHURCHES TO FOLLOW THEIR BLUEPRINT?

The question now naturally arises how the apostles of the early church viewed their authority when it came to establishing church *form* and *function*. Did the apostles view the patterns they modeled as normative for all churches or simply optional? Were believers free to do whatever they wanted when it came to the church?

Below are several excerpts from letters that Paul wrote to churches in the cities of Corinth and Thessalonica that he was directly involved in starting and coaching.[171] Paul is writing to groups with whom he has a personal relationship and, hence, feels some perceived right and responsibility to instruct them. These few key scriptures express how he felt about the practices he and his apostolic co-workers implemented among these communities:

> Now I praise you because you remember me in everything, and hold firmly to the *traditions*, just as I delivered them to you.[172]

> So then, brethren, stand firm and hold to the *traditions* which you were taught, whether by word of mouth or by letter from us.[173]

> But if one is inclined to be contentious, we have *no other practice*, nor have the churches of God.[174]

---

[170] Acts 2:46, 5:42, 20:20; Rom 16:3-5,10,11,14,15
[171] Acts 17:1-4, 18:1-18
[172] 1 Cor 11:2 (NASB, emphasis added)
[173] 2 Thes 2:15 (NASB, emphasis added)
[174] 1 Cor 11:16 (NASB, emphasis added)

Did the word of God originate with you? Or are you the only people it has reached? If anybody thinks he is a prophet or spiritually gifted, let him acknowledge that what I am writing to you is *the Lord's command*. If he ignores this, he himself will be ignored.[175]

Several things are noteworthy. First, in the initial two quotations, Paul congratulates both groups for holding firmly to the 'traditions' he imparted to them either personally or through his letters. The traditions referred to are inherited ways of thinking or behaving. These are not to be confused with the traditions of the Pharisees that Jesus rejected and condemned as being simply human inventions not originating from God.[176] Nor are these 'traditions' (Greek = *paradosis*, meaning ordinance, custom, or precept) simply to be equated with mere 'teachings' (Greek = *didaskalia*, meaning instruction, doctrine, or learning). Rather, the traditions also included patterns and practices that the apostles, as God's messengers, infused into the lives of the churches they founded. They implemented a blueprint for the way churches were to function and the form they were to take.

Second, the immediate context of the third quotation concerns a controversial issue that is beyond the scope of this book, namely head coverings. However, the point Paul is trying to make here is the principle of common practice among all churches that he expected the Corinthian believers to also implement. There were no other alternatives from which to choose. Those who ignored apostolic instructions were considered argumentative and contentious.

Third, the surrounding scriptural context of the opening and last quotations specifically relates to what happens when Christians get together for church meetings. Paul instructed these assemblies to be open, participatory, and interactive gatherings. There were to be no one-man shows. But, they were also clearly meant to have a certain sense of order and flow, rather than be chaotic.

Fourth, the last passage comes at the end of a lengthy discussion by Paul about the open Spirit-led format of church meetings. Obviously, he felt very strongly that the instructions he gave came

---

[175] 1 Cor 14:36-38 (NIV, emphasis added)
[176] Mark 7:5-14

from the Lord himself and were not simply optional suggestions or his own opinions. In fact, the apostle makes the blunt statement that anyone not recognizing this would themselves not be recognized.

CONCLUSIONS

This chapter has attempted to give some biblical understanding of the first-century church as a movement. We have discovered a critical feature of the early Christians: *they minimized the complexity of their forms in order to maximize the effectiveness of their functions.* They kept organization to a minimum as a house church movement so they could focus on their dynamic mandate of making disciples of Christ and expanding into new uncharted territories. The following summarizes the essential elements discussed in this chapter.

Organism

The early Jesus movement identified itself more along the lines of relationships with each other and with Christ, rather than membership in an organization. The numerous metaphors used of a family, a body, a household, a flock, a spiritual temple, etc., indicate that the church was less of a spiritual factory and more of an organic entity. They held to a family and organic theology of the church.

Homes and House-sized Churches

The early church customarily met in private homes in small groups of up to thirty people and, consequently, can be described as a house church movement. It was a 'living room' revolution. Each group was a legitimate church in itself. In addition, there is no archaeological or manuscript evidence for special church buildings for the first 300 years of Christian history. Although they did not necessarily employ the house church form consciously, it was the natural result of their theology of church as family and their belief in the participatory and interactive nature of gatherings. Their house-sized churches were simple, small, natural, intimate, inexpensive, adaptable, duplicatable, and were a breeding ground for new leaders. As such, the apostles organized believers into homes using the principle that 'church *is* small groups'.

Open Meetings

Visiting a first-century house church, one would have immediately noticed the interactive and participatory nature of the gatherings, where everyone had the chance and responsibility to contribute their spiritual gift to the mix. No one-man shows. However, there seemed to have been key elements always present like prayer, the Lord's Supper as a full meal together, teaching, group discussion, tongues, and free prophecy. This, although, was all done simply, interactively, and as the Spirit led.

Leadership

Two primary types of leadership were evident in the early church, namely mobile and local leaders. The mandate of mobile leaders was temporary and universal. Their job description included establishing churches in unreached areas, coaching these churches, and training and appointing local leaders. They usually received some form of financial support for their work. The mandate of local leaders, however, was long term and localized. They worked in co-equal teams to shepherd and direct the activities of individual house churches and the citywide network in their care. They were volunteers who did not receive financial assistance for their ministry.

Connecting as a Movement

House churches were never left to fend for themselves but, rather, were linked together with other clusters of local believers. They were connected primarily in three ways: traveling apostolic teams that circulated from city-to-city to bring encouragement and instruction; house-to-house meeting patterns within a city; and occasional citywide gatherings of house churches, elders, and apostles.

Growth

New Testament believers were actively involved in spreading the message of Jesus Christ throughout the Mediterranean world, both in word and in deed. They were brave and creative even in the face of persecution. They engaged in public proclamation, private conversation, power encounters, and the proliferation of new house churches as they grew.

Apostolic Blueprint

The first apostles and subsequent apostolic workers established the way the early church functioned and organized itself. This was not done whimsically but was based on how God was leading them and on Christ's example. Thus, as they stated clearly, they expected these communities to follow their practices, both in function and form.

QUESTIONS FOR GROUP REFLECTION

1. *Metaphors describing the Church.* Which metaphor in the New Testament used for the church speaks most powerfully to you?

2. *The Location of Early Church Meetings.* Why do you think the early church met primarily in private homes? Which aspects of their theology and practical lifestyle as a community caused them to do so?

3. *The Format of Early Church Meetings.* What major differences stand out to you between what happened during New Testament meetings compared to traditional Sunday morning church services or even in home cell groups today?

4. *Apostles and Elders.* What is the difference between mobile workers (apostles) and local workers (elders)? Which of these two do you think God has gifted you in and/or may be calling you to be?

5. *Apostolic Patterns.* Do you tend to view the 'house church' patterns seen in the New Testament as descriptive or prescriptive? Why?

6. *Apostolic Authority.* How do you view the apostles' authority and their instructions to the churches?

GROUP EXERCISE

Rediscovering Church Together. You will try to experience a New Testament type of meeting. Break your large group up, if necessary, into smaller groups of no more than eight people. Give each group a bag with one Bible, a loaf of bread, and a fake cheque. The only instructions are that each group is to discover how to 'be the church' to one another. Get back together as a large group after 30-45 minutes and report on what happened. (Try this exercise full blast: have an evening together over a meal with no preplanned agenda other than that you will have the Lord's Supper together. See where the Spirit leads).

4

HISTORICAL PERSPECTIVES

HOUSE CHURCH MOVEMENTS, THEN AND NOW

We have just finished probing the New Testament for any deliberate apostolic patterns and practices that existed in the first century Christian church. It is apparent that the early church looked like an expanding network of house churches, a vast sea of little clusters of disciples meeting in homes. Sometimes we modern day believers, especially in the West, thumb through the pages of the New Testament wistfully and longingly for the apparent power and simplicity of those early days. Sometimes we wish we could have been there. Sometimes we wonder when it all changed.

We forget, however, that the house church movement never completely died. To the contrary, house churches not only continued to survive throughout history but, as we shall see, were critical in bringing renewal and reform at key moments to the Body of Christ at large. Even today in many parts of the world there is a move of God through house churches that is beginning to shake church structures and paradigms. As astutely observed by one historian of a bygone era:

> Events in the history of the churches in the time of the apostles have been selected and recorded in the book of Acts in such a way as to provide a permanent pattern for the churches. Departure from this pattern has had disas-

trous consequences, and all revival and restoration have been due to some return to the pattern and principles in the Scriptures.[177]

It is a matter of interest and importance, then, to understand the broader historical and contemporary context to see what lessons can be learned and applied by today's emerging global house church movement.

HOUSE CHURCH MOVEMENTS THEN ...

The First Three Centuries

To recap briefly, we saw in the last chapter that the house church pattern was normative for first century Christians. Jesus, for example, chose twelve to be with him as disciples who would later be sent out as apostles, effectively modeling the type of intimacy, interaction, and involvement only possible in a small discipleship circle. The apostle Peter found himself leading a Jerusalem church numbering in the thousands and meeting almost entirely in private homes soon after Pentecost. The apostle Paul wrote to groups of disciples throughout the Roman Empire, greeting by name those who hosted Christian gatherings in their homes. These house churches felt up-close-and-personal because they were able to accommodate at most thirty-five people comfortably.[178] Meetings were open, interactive, and participatory. Everyone brought something to the 'spiritual table' for the benefit of everyone else. No attractive worship services, expensive programs, church buildings, or professional clergy were needed. It was this kind of simple, small, grassroots, household pattern that persisted and permeated the Roman Empire to the point that five percent of the entire population had become Christian by the early fourth century.[179]

The Fourth Century: A Turning Point

In 313 A.D. the Roman emperor Constantine legalized Christianity and began to institute a number of changes that have affected and

---

[177] E.H. Broadbent, *The Pilgrim Church*, Grand Rapids, MI, USA: Gospel Folio Press, 1999, p.26.

[178] Del Birkey, *The House Church*, Scottdale, PA, USA: Herald Press, 1988, p.55.

[179] John Driver, *Radical Faith: An Alternative History of the Christian Church*, Kitchener, ON, Canada: Pandora Press, 1999, p.42.

afflicted the church to this day. He facilitated the establishment of a professional hierarchical clergy system modeled after Roman government and military systems, the construction of special church buildings, and a political state-church merger. Thus, 'Cathedral' Christianity was born.

The church, perhaps not surprisingly, embraced these moves. After years of toil and persecution, it felt like the Body of Christ had finally beaten the Evil Empire. This was one of the most tragic moments in Christian history. After trying hard to destroy the church by beating it with a stick, Satan now dangled a carrot in front of its eyes. Sadly, this was the moment when the church said 'yes' to the same temptations that Jesus himself said 'no' to in the desert, namely the temptations of power, popularity, and position.

By 380 A.D., the influential bishops Theodosius and Gratian mandated that there should be one state-recognized church that would tell everyone else what to believe and what to do. Private home meetings were effectively outlawed for fear of heresy and splinter groups. What followed over the next 1700 years have been state-run and/or denominational churches often organized and managed more like mini political empires, i.e. Christendom, rather than grassroots communities of believers on a mission from God, i.e. Christianity. Special church buildings now replaced the need for Christian hospitality. Paid clergy now replaced the participation of ordinary believers. Programs and rituals now replaced Spirit-led, open, and passionate meetings. A religious organization now replaced the living Body of Christ. But, gladly, that's not where the story ends.

Pre-Reformation Movements (300 - 1500 A.D.)[180]

Running parallel with this state-run church, however, were numerous reform and renewal movements which flourished over the next millennium: Donatists, Priscillians, Paulicians, Peter Waldo and the Waldensians, Francis of Assisi and the Little Brothers, John Wyclif and the Lollards, Peter Chelcicky and the Czech Brethren, etc. Some attempted to reform the state church, whereas others separated from

---

[180] John Driver, *Radical Faith,* 1999; Wolfgang Simson, *Houses that Change the World*, Carlisle, Cumbria, UK: Paternoster, 1998; E.H. Broadbent, *The Pilgrim Church*, 1999.

it. Some were more orthodox in their doctrine than others. They often advocated pacifism, identified with the poor and marginalized, promoted common people's access to and understanding of the Bible, and advocated for the equality of women. Another common element found in many of these movements was meeting in private homes. Whether this was due to persecution and poverty or from biblical conviction is sometimes difficult to determine. These radical movements, however, continued to challenge the religious establishment in its thinking and practice.

Priscillian (340-385 A.D.)

As a Spanish nobleman of wealth, position, education, and great personal charisma, Priscillian was initially more interested in Greek philosophy than in Christianity. He was eventually converted to Christ, baptized, and began a life of serious devotion to God. He became a diligent student of the Bible and began to preach and teach, although only a layman. He initiated a lay movement of 'brotherhoods' throughout Spain and France in which only converted and baptized believers could participate. These meetings were primarily Bible reading sessions, with both men and women participating. He was joined by a large number of bishops and priests in rebelling against the state church by asserting the independence of each local congregation. There were false accusations that Priscillian espoused a kind of Gnostic-Manichaean dualism, which taught that physical matter was evil. In this view, all of humanity was trapped, the way to salvation being the renunciation of the material world and the embrace of the spiritual. The Roman Emperor Maximus did not like the tensions that existed between the state church and this faction. He eventually had Priscillian and six of his friends arrested and beheaded in Trier, France, to the great protest of Priscillian's former opponents, the eminent bishops Martin of Tours and Ambrose of Milan. The bodies were brought back to Spain where they were hailed as martyrs. After Priscillian's death the movement, although persecuted, grew such that it took two centuries to stamp it out completely.

Peter Waldo (1150-1206)

Waldo was from Lyon, France, and belonged to the emerging urban class of merchants and artisans trying to find a niche for itself within the traditional feudal system. He developed an interest in the gospel accounts of Christ's life and employed a monk to translate a number of biblical selections into the vernacular. After much reading and study he became convinced that he could no longer take part in the grab for power and money his peers were engaged in. He eventually renounced his wealth and felt that only those who embraced apostolic poverty could in good conscience preach the gospel message. Waldo's followers, known as the Poor Ones of Lyon or Waldensians, were dedicated to itinerant preaching tours, traveling two by two throughout the French countryside. They expanded their work all over Europe, so much so that it was believed by the canon of Notre Dame that a third of all Christendom had attended the Waldensian meetings. Their gatherings usually occurred outdoors after nightfall under the direction of an itinerant brother. After an opening prayer and sermon, they went back into their homes for supper meetings to pray, discuss, and eat the Lord's Supper. Their mission flew in the face of the vision for society administered by church and civil authorities. The Waldensians prohibited taking oaths, encouraged people to voluntarily renounce wealth, organized among its followers an alternate economic system to state sponsored feudalism, refused to participate in all forms of violence, questioned much of the established church's teachings and practices, and made great inroads among the poor, the uneducated, and women. After Waldo's death, the Roman Catholic Church condemned the Waldensian movement outright at the Fourth Lateran Council (1215), promptly excommunicating and punishing those who disobeyed.

Post-Reformation Movements[181]

Most Protestant Christians—mainline, evangelical, and charismatic—gaze back fondly at the turbulent years of the 16th century as a time of theological purification of the state sponsored Roman Catholic church in Western Europe. This period in church history is referred to as the 'Reformation'. Although the so-called Reformers instigated significant rediscoveries in faith (i.e. theology), they left previous Roman Catholic church structures (i.e. ecclesiology) almost completely intact and patterned them into the new Reformed

---

[181] John Driver, *Radical Faith*, 1999; Peter Bunton, *Cell Groups and House Churches: What History Teaches Us*, Ephrata, PA, USA: House to House Publications, 2001; Wolfgang Simson, *Houses that Change the World*, 1998; E.H. Broadbent, *The Pilgrim Church*, 1999.

churches. But, not everyone was satisfied that the changes went far enough. Enter the radical wing of the Reformation. They sounded a clarion call to get back to the basics of church form and function, opening up a Pandora's box that more moderate Reformers were ill prepared to face. As we shall see, ironically, it was moderates like Luther and Zwingli—who were themselves once at odds with the Roman Catholic state-run church—that became the oppressors and critics of the so-called radicals who wanted to cut even deeper into the heart of the problems that plagued the church by getting back to apostolic practices and not just apostolic theology.

Martin Luther (1483-1546)

This famous German Reformer realized that reforms could be taken even further. He suggested that a third order of service in private homes[182] should supplement the public Latin and German language masses. The purpose of these groups was to engage in prayer, Bible reading, baptism, the Lord's Supper, mutual accountability, and collecting money for the poor. Luther, though, refused to pursue the idea for fear of the potential divisiveness of such groups, which could start claiming they were the only true Christians. Moreover, he did not believe he would be able to find other people interested in such an idea. Luther would later go so far as to even deride and persecute those who promoted home gatherings as being dangerous dissenters.

Caspar von Schwenckfeld (1490-1561)

An influential nobleman, Schwenckfeld was engaged in matters of business and did not show any interest in the Christian faith well into his adulthood. At the age of 30, he had a spiritual awakening after coming into contact with Luther's teachings and soon became the heart and soul of the Reformation in his native Silesia. Initially a favourite disciple of Luther's, Schwenckfeld became an outlawed Reformer and officially labeled a heretic because of strong disagreements with his mentor. Schwenckfeld's earnest desire was to use the Scriptures to reform the church's beliefs and practices: "If we would reform the Church, we must make use of the Holy Scriptures and especially of Acts, where it is clearly to be found how things were in the beginning, what is right and what is wrong, what is praiseworthy

---

[182] Martin Luther, preface to *The German Mass and Order of Service*, 1526.

and acceptable to God and to the Lord Christ."[183] As such, he pleaded with Luther to turn away from his nearly Roman Catholic ecclesiology, to which Luther responded with severe denunciation and persecution.

For the remaining thirty years of his life Schwenckfeld became a wanted man in Europe, fleeing persecution by Lutheran preachers, all the while starting home fellowship groups that focused on prayer and Bible study. To avoid further aggravating his pursuers, he did not encourage baptism or the Lord's Supper in these gatherings. After his death, Lutheran pastors attempted to coerce Schwenckfeld's numerous followers back into officially recognized state-run churches, jailing those who refused.

Juan de Valdes (1500-1541)

A young man of Jewish descent, Valdes became the key player in advancing the lay movement in Spain and Italy known as 'Evangelism' or 'Valdesianism'. In his early twenties, Valdes participated in one of the small group gatherings led by Pedro Ruiz de Alcaraz, who dedicated himself to teaching the Bible in people's homes. These meetings were informal, involved the participation of both men and women, and attracted a large number of Jews and other social outsiders. Valdes was influenced by the radical ecclesiological vision of Alcaraz, who was opposed to many of the Roman Catholic Church's sacramental, hierarchical, and doctrinal systems.

Valdes would later write a widely read book entitled *Dialogo de Doctrina Cristiana*, which encapsulated his beliefs about the need for Church reform and Christian faith. In 1531, the Inquisition confiscated copies of his books, forbade their reading, and launched an investigation of Valdes, causing him to flee to Italy. During these last ten years of his life, he founded a community in Naples that met in private homes on Sundays for Bible study and prayer and was united in its concern for the poor. Although Valdes attracted many persons of renown from the religious and social world, his ideas also permeated the marketplace where tanners could be overheard discussing the Pauline epistles. Approximately 3,000 people came to be associated with the Italian movement, whose members fled or were executed when the Papal Inquisition was re-instated.

---

[183] E.H. Broadbent, *The Pilgrim Church*, p.214.

The Anabaptists (c.1520)[184]

This movement found its roots in the circle of radical disciples that gathered around the ex-Catholic priest and Swiss Reformer Ulrich Zwingli. As Zwingli studied the Bible, he came to the conclusion that many traditional Catholic practices were in error. He broke with the papacy and was then established by Zurich city council as the official city pastor. His fervent preaching inspired the common people to demand changes not only in government taxation policies, but also in the church's liturgical patterns. Zwingli's demands for sweeping changes in the church were rejected time and again by city council, causing him to eventually back down. This disillusioned many of his most ardent followers and friends, particularly Conrad Grebel and Felix Mantz, who went on to establish an illegal church near Zurich. The pair, along with the fiery ex-priest George Blaurock, began to organize clandestine home meetings where biblical passages were read and discussed and the Lord's Supper shared. This dissident group also began to rebaptize adults who had only been baptized as infants, believing their current practice to be more biblical. Within six months, the movement had found its way to neighbouring towns and cities, into other regions in the Swiss confederation, and eventually into Germany. These rebaptizers, or Anabapstists, met with both denunciation and persecution from Zwingli and government authorities. Conrad Grebel, worn down by a lengthy imprisonment followed by escape and strenuous travel, died from the plague. Felix Mantz was eventually arrested and drowned by the authorities. George Blaurock was burned at the stake. However, by the end of the century, Anabaptists could be found in Austria, Moravia, Slovakia, and Hungary, numbering in the tens of thousands.

Jean de Labadie (1610-1674)

Ordained a Jesuit priest in 1635, Labadie tried without success to reform the Catholic Church until 1650. He shifted allegiances and became a Protestant minister and theology professor, trying unsuccessfully for the next twenty years to bring the Protestant church back to apostolic patterns. Eventually he realized that his

---

[184] C. Arnold Snyder, *Anabaptist History and Theology*, Kitchener, ON, Canada: Pandora Press, 1995; J.A. Moore, *Anabaptist Portraits*, Herald Press, 1984.

energies would be served best by starting something completely fresh outside the constraints of both Roman Catholicism and Protestantism. He envisioned a day when all Christians would abandon their rites and ceremonies in favour of the simplicity of the early church. In Amsterdam, thousands of people gathered around him to establish a community based on this radical vision. The Reformed Church in Holland was particularly opposed to the spontaneous prayers Labadie endorsed among his followers. Labadie also established groups called 'conventicles' or 'brotherhoods' in France and Switzerland. He wrote the first 'how to' book[185] for these home gatherings, giving very practical advice regarding prayer, singing, Bible study, discussion, and free prophecy. Labadie did not bow to the authority of the Reformed Church in Holland, refused to sign the Belgic Confession, and was eventually excommunicated.

George Fox (1624-1691)

Fox, the founder of the Quakers (also called Friends), grew up in a very religious home and spent his late teens and early twenties traveling throughout England sharing his concerns about the practices of the established churches, but without much success. After a profound spiritual experience involving a vision on Pendle Hill in which he saw a great crowd of people who would receive his message, he rapidly began to gain a hearing by his preaching efforts. He summarized his mission in his autobiography:

> I declared unto them that the Lord God had sent me to preach the everlasting gospel and word of life amongst them, and to bring them off from all these temples, tithes, priests, and rudiments of the world, which had been instituted since the apostles' days, and had been set up by such as had erred from the Spirit and power the apostles were in.[186]

Many of the early Quakers went out two by two and began traveling throughout England and eventually the world, drawing 20,000 converts in the first five years of their mission and attracting severe persecution from religious and civil authorities. The Quakers emphasized the work of the Spirit in a believer's life, the inner light

---

[185] *The Discernment of a True Church According to the Holy Scriptures Containing Thirty Remarkable Signs by Which it May Be Well Known*
[186] George Fox, *Journal*, Chapter VI.

and seed in each person, personal piety, open Spirit-led church meetings, complete pacifism, solidarity with the poor and ordinary workers, equality between the sexes, and opposition to both Catholic and Protestant 'steeple houses' and clergy systems. To eliminate false distinctions between sacred and secular places of worship, they preached in the open air and met in homes.

Philip Jacob Spener (1635-1705)

Spener, the founder of Pietism and a student of Jean de Labadie, sought to reform the increasingly scholastic and sterile German Lutheran church by emphasizing personal spiritual experience. His main strategy was to supplement Sunday morning services with small home groups called 'pious gatherings' in which the priesthood of all believers would be practiced. Pastors or professors would serve as qualified facilitators of these groups, whose focus was discipleship and holiness. Because Spener did not want to upset the establishment and did not see these small groups as replacing but only supplementing traditional church services, he would not permit baptism or the Lord's Supper. Spener's first group was eventually suppressed in his hometown of Frankfurt, after which he became cynical and decided not to start any new groups. However, through his book *Pia Desideria* (meaning 'Pious Desires'), his influence was felt by both the Moravians and Methodists, who in turn had a major role during the 18th century Great Awakening.

John Wesley (1703-1791)[187]

As an Anglican priest, Wesley began his religious career in various parishes. Several years later, he returned to Oxford and joined his brother Charles and friend George Whitefield in a small circle for accountability, prayer, Bible study, communion, and works of charity. After an unfruitful stint as a missionary to the American state of Georgia, Wesley returned to England in a deep spiritual depression. Following a series of inner experiences in which he felt spiritually empowered, Wesley began to preach outdoors to crowds, something frowned upon in that day.

---

[187] Howard Snyder, *The Radical Wesley and Patterns for Church Renewal*, Downers Grove, IL, USA: InterVarsity Press, 1980; John Driver, *Radical Faith*, 1999.

Over the next fifty years, he sought to gather the thousands of converts from his outdoor preaching into cell groups of six to twelve people for accountability, discipleship, care for the sick, and collecting money in support of the poor. In fact, Wesley refused to preach in any area unless he was permitted to organize converts into cell groups with adequate leadership installed. The lay leaders of these clusters, both men and women, acted as pastors and disciplers. The 'classes' and 'bands' themselves functioned somewhat like house churches, meeting in the neighbourhood homes of members. They would also gather together regularly as a corporate body (i.e. 'society') for lecture-type teaching and hymn singing; however, only members of cell groups were permitted to attend these large group 'society' gatherings.

Circuit riders would flow from city-to-city to bring cohesion to the movement. Meetings were scheduled not to interfere with traditional Anglican services because of Wesley's desire to bring about renewal within the Anglican Church, rather than create a separate movement. At John Wesley's death in 1791, the Methodist movement in Britain and the United States was composed of approximately 10,000 home cell groups and over 100,000 people.

... AND HOUSE CHURCH MOVEMENTS NOW

Today, there is a massive influx into the Body of Christ through house churches. In fact, it has been suggested that there are more Christians involved in house churches around the world today than in any other kind of church. The following is simply one tiny snapshot, the tip of an iceberg, of what is happening around the world in these modern times.

China[188]

There has been a long history of missionary effort by both Protestants and Catholics in the land of the dragon, helping establish the

---

[188] Tony Lambert, *China's Christian Millions*, London, UK: Monarch Books, 1999; Larry Kreider, *House Church Networks*, House to House Publications, 2001; Dennis McCallum, "Watchman Nee and the House Church Movement in China", www.xenos.org/essays/nee1.htm, 1986; Patrick Johnstone and Jason Mandryk, *Operation World*, WEC International, www.wec-int.org, 2001.

spiritual groundwork for future generations of indigenous Christian leaders.

After the communist revolution in 1949, almost all foreign missionaries and diplomats were expelled. Estimates were that there were perhaps only one to two million Christians at the time, leaving many Western believers thinking China was a lost cause spiritually.

The government established a policy of sanctioning registered churches under the umbrella of the 'Three-Self Patriotic Movement' (TSPM), which advocated the principles of self-support, self-administration, and self-propagation. Although this was apparently designed to eliminate Chinese churches from control of foreign religious agencies, TSPM churches had their own activities curtailed by the government.

By 1966, China's Red Guards closed the few remaining churches, forcing believers to go underground for the next thirteen years. Those who refused to register and engaged in preaching activities faced arrest and imprisonment.

In 1972, the same year that U.S. President Nixon visited China, reports started streaming out about the clandestine activities of the underground church.

Under the liberalization of President Deng Xiaoping, church buildings were once again re-opened in 1979. After his death in 1997, several years of tightening control and forced registration of house churches followed. This increase in pressure caused leaders of ten major house church networks, comprising tens of millions of believers, to send a united written appeal to the Chinese authorities to cease persecution and open dialogue with house church leaders.

Today, Chinese house church leaders have made a commitment that, even if complete political freedom were to arrive tomorrow, there would be certain aspects of church structure and function they would keep intact.

Specifically, contemporary leaders have decided to: (a) encourage leaders to be mobile evangelizers and house church planters; (b) model teamwork; (c) *not* build any church buildings; (d) continue to have a mobile 'tabernacle' mentality rather than a stationary 'temple' mindset; and (e) only provide financial support to traveling apostolic workers while local leaders remain volunteers.

Current estimates suggest between 80 and 130 million Christian believers.[189] China has for decades now been the prime modern day example of how the simplicity of house churches provides the ideal vehicle for church growth even under adverse circumstances.

India

There are approximately 30 million Christians in India, with another 70 million secret believers who have been afraid to join visible churches because of opposition. However, many believers have joined house churches because of their low visibility and indigenous nature.

One such movement of house churches started as recently as 1995.[190] Dr. Victor Choudhrie, a well-known surgeon, and his wife Bindu started an experiment that did not involve paid clergy, church buildings, or even Sunday services. They began deploying church planters, mostly lower-caste young men with little training, into the central Indian state of Madhya Pradesh. In a few short years, Choudhrie estimates that 3,500 house churches have been planted numbering 70,000 people. Their vision is to eventually plant a house church in every one of the 17,000 villages of Madhya Pradesh by the year 2007.[191]

Just north in the state of Uttar Pradesh, comparable phenomenal growth occurred during 2001 with 1,250 brand new house churches planted and 6,000 believers willing to be trained further.[192] Many of these house churches begin as Christians—many less than two years in the faith—engage in door-to-door evangelism campaigns offering to pray for people.[193] Healings and demonic deliverance are not uncommon, resulting in families opening up their homes to become

---

[189] Actual estimates of China's Christian population vary from sources in the previous footnote: Tony Lambert (17 million); Larry Kreider (80 million); Johnstone and Mandryk (91 million); James Rutz in a private communication suggested to me a much higher estimate (130 million).

[190] James Rutz with Victor Choudhrie, "House Church Explosion in India", House-2-House Magazine, Issue 2, 2002, www.house2house.tv

[191] Larry Kreider, *House Church Networks*, p.33.

[192] Friday Fax, "Uttar Pradesh: Over 1000 New Churches Planted Last Year", Issue 23, June 7, 2002, fridayfax@bufton.net

[193] Friday Fax, "Thousands of Hindus find Jesus in Houses of Prayer", Issue 31, August 2, 2002, fridayfax@bufton.net

'houses of prayer', which then become multiplying house churches. Thousands have come to faith in Christ in this way.

There are similar movements sprouting up all over India.

Ethiopia[194]

In 1974 a Marxist regime was installed as the government of Ethiopia. By 1982 the charismatic Meserete Kristos Church was completely outlawed, with its buildings confiscated and its key leaders arrested. This began an almost decade long government repression of the church. Leaders who had escaped the crackdown met secretly to discuss their options and decided to organize church members into small home groups of five to seven people to pray, sing, study the Bible, discuss, and have the Lord's Supper together. Along with obtaining maps to organize these groups according to geography, the leaders prepared study materials for group leaders.

At first, members were uncomfortable with the idea because of the cultural practice of using their homes only for family and social activities, not religious ones. However, the idea caught on and an underground house church movement was born. Because of the illegality of preaching publicly, believers used funerals and weddings, in particular, as opportunities to talk to people about Christ. They also had musicians travel from house to house to bring worship music into the home church meetings.

By 1991, the government had been overthrown, allowing the church to come above ground from its hiding place. To the astonishment of everyone, the Kristos church in ten years had grown from 5,000 to 50,000 members. With their buildings now returned, the Kristos believers reorganized themselves into 53 congregations, committed themselves to keeping the small home group structure they had accidentally discovered, and started making plans to evangelize the entire country.

Britain[195]

The 1970s in Britain saw the emergence of an attempt to restore New Testament principles to church life. This movement was based on the

---

[194] "Against Great Odds" (video), Gateway Films, 1992.
[195] Wolfgang Simson, *Houses That Change the World*, pp.72-73; Jonathan Petre, "Christianity in Crisis as Pews Empty", www.telegraph.co.uk, Nov 28, 1999.

discovery that believer's spiritual gifts could not be used effectively in traditional churches. Groups of people began to move out of traditional settings into homes and the outdoors.

However, the use of private homes for their meetings was actually based on circumstances rather than theological conviction. Once the movement began to grow, instead of multiplying into more and more homes, many simply moved into school gyms, community centres, and rented halls. Thus, they went the way of church growth rather than church planting. Although the rediscovery of spiritual gifts renewed qualitative aspects of church life, church structures themselves were left untouched. The end result was that many of these churches simply returned to the old way of doing things.

Even so, during the 1990's, there was 38% growth among these so-called 'New Churches', which includes house churches. This was the largest numerical increase in the U.K. of any Protestant evangelical group during that decade, the next runner up being a 2% spurt among the Baptists. It has been estimated that one third of all evangelicals in Britain are currently part of this movement.

Brazil[196]

A Roman Catholic variant of house churches, commonly termed BCCs (Basic Christian Communities) and BECs (Basic Ecclesial Communities), has seen explosive growth over the past 40 years in the Latin American nation of Brazil. With the overthrow of fascism in 1945 and the greater political openness that followed, the emergence of popular movements was enabled. However, this came to a sudden end in the early 1960s after a successful military coup that curtailed any type of public gatherings or political dissent.

At this juncture, it was the Catholic Church—in the wake of the 'openness to change' embraced by the Second Vatican Council—that provided the only forum for people to gather, find support, and plan what to do in the face of unfolding circumstances. This was the seedbed for the initial formation of small Christian communities. They were birthed to face off the realities of poverty in the lives of the participants, including the elderly, the unemployed, indigenous peoples, peasants, labourers, over-crowded city dwellers, and youth

---

[196] Jeanne Hinton, *Walking in the Same Direction: A New Way of Being Church*, Geneva: WCC Publications, 1995.

frustrated by lack of opportunity. These groups gave voice to the concerns of those at the fringes of society, convinced that God was indeed with them.

Organizationally, these clusters were comprised of about 40 people, were usually led by a priest or trained layperson, and normally had some affiliation with and received support from an already established local Catholic parish. These BCCs met regularly to pray, read the Bible, reflect on their lives, and plan ways to address some of the social injustices in their community, including poverty, labour issues, and the position of women. On many levels, these clusters of people were social experiments that tested out whether faith and life could indeed intersect.

The growth of BCCs in Brazil has been rapid since their inception in the 1960s, numbering 40,000 groups by 1974 and 100,000 groups by 1985.

Cuba[197]

Various political and economic factors brought about Cuba's worst petrol crisis in 1992, causing a virtual traffic standstill. This forced the island's Protestant Christian leaders to appeal to the government on behalf of church members who could no longer afford to travel the ten to fifteen kilometres to attend church on Sunday mornings. Their idea was to reorganize local congregations into neighbourhood house churches within easy reach of believers. The government's only restriction was that these house groups had to be within five kilometres of the original church building. The result by the year 2000 was the emergence of between 6,000 and 10,000 house churches scattered all over Cuba, within walking distance of nearly every Cuban. It is estimated that there is one house church for every 1500 people. Some of these house churches are led by ordained pastors, but mostly it is part-time preachers and teachers traveling from group to group that are helping fuel the revival in Cuba.

North America

Christians gathering in homes and calling it 'church' is slowly but surely gaining popularity in North America. It has been estimated

---

[197] Friday Fax, "Cuba: petrol crisis helps church growth - thanks, Castro!", Issue 20, May 25, 2001, fridayfax@bufton.net; Mindy Belz, "Su Casa es Mi Casa", *World Magazine*, vol.13, no.5, Feb 6, 1998.

that there are about 200 house churches in Canada and about 1500 in the United States.[198] The motivation has been the need for basic Christian community that many have not been able to find within larger impersonal traditional congregations. Many of these home churches have chosen not to register with the government or connect themselves with a denomination, some out of theological conviction and some out of sheer reaction against the control of traditional church establishment. But, fortunately, many house churches are beginning to recognize their need for connecting with each other, with a number of relational and resource networks springing up locally, regionally, and nationally.

Canada. The Canadian House Church Resource Network[199], an arm of the Evangelical Fellowship of Canada, is bringing nationwide awareness and connection by publishing a newsletter, organizing regional and national consultation groups, and advertising the speaking tours of well-known house church consultants like Wolfgang Simson and Robert Fitts. Even some denominations and mission organizations are getting in on the action. The Free Methodist Church in Canada is sponsoring house church planting efforts in two provinces, British Columbia and Ontario, in which this author is involved.[200] The Foursquare Gospel Church of Canada is the first denomination to appoint a director dedicated to overseeing their house churches.[201] The Navigators, a well-respected international organization with years of small group experience, is also considering developing a house church wing to its ministry in Canada. This author has been in consultation with Navigator leadership to see how this could take place.

United States. A number of networks and resource agencies have been established. Robert Fitts, an internationally recognized authority on the topic, has the mandate to identify key people in each state who will take on statewide responsibility for house church

---

[198] Rick Hiebert, "There's no Church like Home", *The Report*, May 28, 2001, p.47.
[199] Canadian House Church Resource Network, www.outreach.ca/cpc/housechurches.htm
[200] The Free Methodist Church in Canada, www.fmc-canada.org
[201] The Foursquare Gospel Church of Canada, www.foursquare.ca/hbcn.htm

planting.[202] Fitts has also established three other 'Hs' to complement the house churches he is involved with: home Bible colleges, houses of prayer, and houses of healing. Tony and Felicity Dale have become major players on the scene by establishing a widely read magazine called *House to House*.[203] Other well-known American figures include Steve Atkerson, Robert Banks, Del Birkey, Gene Edwards, Nate Krupp, Jim Rutz, and Frank Viola. Denominations and so-called para-church organizations are also involved. The Southern Baptist Convention, one of the largest Protestant denominations, is actively planting house churches and cell groups and, as a result, is seeing church planting movements take place among many people groups in Asia and Latin America.[204] Dove Christian Fellowship, known mostly for its cell-group churches, is now embracing and supporting the house church movement as a genuine work of God.[205] Mission organizations such as Campus Crusade for Christ have been planting 'home fellowship groups' for years in various parts of the world, which have really been back-to-basics churches.[206]

All of these efforts can shine a positive light on house churches as a valid effort in the eyes of the broader Christian community.

LESSONS FOR TODAY

Some important lessons for us today can be learned from the history of house church movements, past and present.

Early Church Example

During its first three centuries Christianity was a vast network of small discipleship circles that met in homes. They were connected and fueled by local volunteer leaders, traveling circuit riders, and a citywide church mentality. That this was a normative pattern modeled by the apostles is clearly seen in the New Testament. As

---

[202] Robert Fitts Ministries, www.robertfitts.com
[203] House to House Magazine, www.house2house.tv
[204] David Garrison, *Church Planting Movements*, Southern Baptist Convention, Richmond, VA, USA, www.imb.org, 1999.
[205] Dove Christian Fellowship, www.dcfi.org; Larry Kreider, *House Church Networks*, 2001.
[206] Robert Fitts, *Saturation Church Planting*, Last Days Ministries, 1994, pp.71-78.

such, today's Christian leaders, especially those involved in church planting and church growth efforts, should reconsider their ministries in light of apostolic practices.

Exponential Growth

Because of the multiplying nature of house churches various renewal and revival movements throughout history were able to spread rapidly across entire continents. Today, there is an increased desire among many to fulfill the Great Commission. In the face of today's global population growth, we need to get smaller to grow bigger and move outside the walls of church buildings.

Efficiency

Because house churches are simple, inexpensive, and adaptable, movements by default made use of them, freeing themselves up from building and program maintenance to concentrate on the weightier matters of evangelism and discipleship. This was especially true in regions characterized by persecution and poverty. The most rapid church planting movements today deliberately multiply and plant house churches (and cell groups), challenging us to rethink traditional ideas of the essential elements needed for successful church planting.

Equal Opportunity

Since the Reformation there has been mainly a theoretical assent to the biblical principle of the priesthood of all believers. With their participative and interactive nature, house churches were able to practically release so-called lay people to utilize their spiritual gifts. As well, passionate Christian lay people sparked many of the movements, today viewed positively, with little if any formal theological training. Today's church can follow this example by releasing leaders to start and lead house churches that release all believers to fully use their skills and talents.

Economics

Many of the movements examined were characterized by renunciation of wealth, solidarity with the poor and marginalized, and/or the establishment of communal economic systems for its members as an alternative to existing feudalism. Impoverished believers were, thus, able to benefit from the even wealth distribution of a Christian need-based approach. Today's western church, in contrast, has absorbed a capitalistic mindset driven by the motto 'bigger is better', which needs to be re-evaluated in light of the biblical mandate for social justice. Because house churches are an inexpensive way of doing church, they can funnel a higher proportion of their resources towards such efforts than conventional congregations.

Entropy

House churches have historically always been involved in relational accountability networks with others of like mind to maintain health (doctrinal and behavioral) and prevent instability (scattering and insularity). This, however, did not always eliminate the severe antagonism between house churches and the traditional church. Neither did it bring any real legitimacy to home churches in the eyes of the broader Christian community. Because autonomous groups are sometimes precursors to cults and sects, house churches today should still continue to network with each other. Today's Christians will hopefully learn from the past and welcome the emergence of the phenomenon as a divinely initiated agent for the health of the entire Body of Christ, rather than persecuting it as in times past.

Essential Elements of a Movement

There are three major elements common to most of these movements that not only kept them connected but also dynamically growing. Once they lost sight of any of the three, they would eventually begin to decline. These elements included: (a) Renewal in the form of a deep personal inner life fueled by prayer, empowerment of the Holy Spirit, and radical obedience to God, (b) Reform by way of simple, natural, inexpensive, adaptable, and duplicatable organizational structures such as house churches, local volunteer leaders that shepherded the house groups, and traveling apostolic workers that acted as circuit riders flowing from group-to-group and city-to-city, and (c) Revival in the form of persistent and intentional public and private evangelism.

QUESTIONS FOR GROUP REFLECTION

1. *Constantine.* What, in your opinion, were the positive and/or negative consequences of legalizing Christianity in the fourth century? Should the Church have responded differently to the Emperor Constantine's gifts of money, erection of church buildings, and establishment of a professional class of clergy?

2. *Heroes of History.* Which of the stories or individuals related in this chapter grabbed you the most? Why?

3. *Renewal, Reform, and Revival.* What do you make of the statement that 'The history of the Christian Church is simply the story of the struggle between prophetic and institutional religion'?

4. *House Churches in your Backyard.* Do you think it's possible to see an explosive 'house church movement' happen in your part of the world? What are the favourable circumstances in, and/or obstacles to, making it a reality?

GROUP EXERCISE

Get together and watch a documentary covering house church movements occurring around the world today (see 'Recommended Resources' for details on the videos *Against Great Odds* and *Church Planting Movements*).

5

RADICAL PRINCIPLES
10 DECLARATIONS OF
THE RADICAL CHURCH

Biblical and historical foundations have been laid for the house church movement in the previous chapters. But, how does this affect those feeling called by God today to recapture the lost vision of the radical New Testament church? The following ten statements are meant to be positive declarations of grassroots Christianity as found especially in the emerging global house church movement. They are *not* primarily meant to be criticisms of more traditional and institutionalized segments of the church, since we embrace all who know, love, and follow Jesus Christ as our genuine brothers and sisters. These declarations, rather, are a call to revolution, *not* reaction and rejection! They are a call to a *renewal* of the church by a radical passion for and obedience to Jesus Christ. They are a call to a *reform* of church structures back to the apostolic and biblical model of church. They are a call to a *revival* of the planet's responsiveness to the person of Christ. They are a challenge to all of us who are Christians to become more biblical and, as a result, more practical, effective, and strategic. These ten declarations are guideposts for the radical church of tomorrow!

DECLARATION 1
We Declare a Present God vs. an Absent God

For too long, God has been seen by many as a disinterested, aloof, distant, absent, 'somewhere-out-there', impersonal force. But, the tide is turning! We now declare that God is a personal, intelligent, and compassionate being who is passionate about us as individuals and as a human race (John 3:16).

God, time and again, rolls up his sleeves and gets down to business with us in the muck and mire, the beauty and virtue, of our world. His ultimate expression of this was when he came to earth in person, face-to-face, in the flesh, as the man Jesus Christ. He lived, loved, taught, healed, cried, laughed, gathered followers, went to a cruel death on a Roman cross to absorb all the darkness of human sin, and three days later rose from the dead. Through this experience on earth, he showed his solidarity with us. He discovered what it's like to be you and me (Philip 2:5-8; Heb 4:15). And now we know what God is like (John 1:14). He is accessible to all people every-where, at all times, in all nations, by a personal faith encounter with Jesus Christ (Rom 1:16; Gal 3:26-28).

God is, in a word, present.

DECLARATION 2

We Declare an Apostolic Heritage vs. Man-made Institutions

For too long, we Christians have been primarily identifying ourselves with man-made institutions and denominations, especially Roman Catholic, Eastern Orthodox, Anglican, and Protestant. But, the tide is turning! We now declare that grassroots Christianity is best lived outside institutions by going back to the apostolic heritage of the New Testament era in both faith *and* practice, function *and* form (1 Cor 11:2; 2 Thes 2:15).

To be sure, we affirm the ways God has, is, and will continue to find ways to work within institutional structures and among our genuine brothers and sisters found there. But, we also challenge and encourage the institutional church to leave many of its unbiblical practices and get back to the basics of apostolic Christianity.

Is there an apostolic pattern found in the Bible for church form and function that transcends culture, time, and language? We in the house church movement believe the answer is a resounding "Yes"! So, for our part, we find kindred spirits especially in those people movements in history who stepped beyond institutional limitations, to one degree or another, in order to restore New Testament beliefs *and* practices. They were variously called Priscillians, Waldensians, Lollards, Huguenots, Anabaptists, Quakers, Moravians, Methodists, Brethren, etc.

DECLARATION 3

We Declare a Relevant Mission vs. a Religious Mission

For too long, we Christians have engaged the world in "religious" ways, placing a wedge between body and spirit, sacred and secular, church and world, church and para-church, Great Commandment and Great Commission, loving God and loving people. But, the tide is turning! We now declare a grassroots Christianity that engages the world with the great news of Christ in a relevant way that can transform entire neighbourhoods, cities, and nations.

To do this, the veil creating these artificial divides must be torn down. We must take the church to the world, rather than expecting the world to come to the church (Acts 1:8). We must engage the world on its own terms, rather than isolate ourselves (1 Cor 9:19-23). We must care for people's physical needs and spiritual needs, rather than pitting one against the other (Mat 25:31-46). We must make disciples of Christ, rather than simply getting decisions for Christ (Mat 28:19-20).

DECLARATION 4

We Declare a Grassroots Church vs. State-Church Partnership

For too long, we Christians have been intertwined with the governments of the world, sometimes by accident, sometimes deliberately. But, the tide is turning! We now declare that true grassroots Christianity is best lived out by a complete separation of church and state (Mat 4:8-10; John 6:15, 17:14-18, 18:36; Acts 17:7; Rom 12:2; 2 Cor 10:3-4; Eph 6:12; James 4:4; 1 John 5:19).

From the time of Constantine in the fourth century, the ties between various churches and the state have been strong politically, militarily, economically, and culturally. This has only served to pollute the purity and dilute the power of the church in carrying out its real mandate of making disciples of Christ. The historic consequences have come in the form of medieval military crusades, inquisitions, persecutions, and modern conflicts all waged under a religious banner. Perhaps even worse, these have served to impede, if not completely ruin, Christianity's witness and work among many people groups.

True change among the nations will only come from a grassroots Christianity that speaks prophetically with God's power and authority, rather than by virtue of any state-sponsored influence.

DECLARATION 5

We Declare the Citywide Church vs. Denominations

For too long, we Christians have been separated from each other and divided along denominational lines like corporations, organizations, or political bodies with branch offices in various towns, cities, and nations. But, the tide is turning! We now declare a grassroots Christianity that works together strategically as a citywide church in order to effectively reach that city or region as was done in the New Testament era (Acts 9:31, 15:36, 20:17; Rom 1:7; 1 Cor 1:2; 2 Cor 1:1; Gal 1:2; Eph 1:1; Philip 1:1; Col 1:2; 1 Thes 1:1; 2 Thes 1:1).

Denominationalism, unfortunately, has historically often served to fragment Christians into different camps even within the same geographic locality, effectively crippling them from reaching out as a united Body of Christ. Fortunately, God is working mightily today to break down many of these barriers to unify Christians to maximize their efforts to disciple their city for Christ.

Therefore, as grassroots radical Christians, we in the house church movement encourage efforts that prioritize citywide church efforts over any existing denominational ties.

DECLARATION 6

We Declare Common People vs. Holy Clergy

For too long, we Christians have promoted the professionalization of Christian leadership. This religious caste system has created a rift between so-called clergy and laity, often resulting in a lack of involvement by lay people. But, the tide is turning! We now declare a grassroots Christianity that rightfully and practically restores the biblical priesthood of all 'common' believers (1 Pet 2:4-10).

All believers can discover, use, and sharpen their spiritual gifts, talents, and capacities for the benefit of the entire Body of Christ (Rom 12:4-8; 1 Cor 12:7-12,27-30). All believers can facilitate even the most sacred symbolic acts, namely the Lord's Supper and Baptism, traditionally carried out only by ordained clergy. All believers are ministers in the truest sense and have a God-given ministry to carry out. There is no such thing as a priest or minister, for all Christians are believer-priests.

We, therefore, encourage a shift away from the unbiblical, professionalized, hierarchical, and money-draining clergy system, whether pope, cardinal, bishop, priest, minister, pastor, or senior elder. We suggest, instead, a return to New Testament forms of leadership, namely local teams of co-equal elders (volunteers) and traveling apostolic teams (financially supported when needed) (Acts 13:1-3, 14:23, 17:9-15, 20:1-6, 20:17,33-35; 1 Cor 9:1-18; Titus 1:5-9). These are grassroots leaders who have been trained and approved by the Body of Christ.

DECLARATION 7
We Declare Common Meetings vs. Holy Rituals

For too long, we Christians have been performing choreographed and polished ceremonies and holy rituals and calling it church. But, the tide is turning! We now declare a return to the clear New Testament practice of having Spirit-led, open, participatory, and interactive 'common' meetings where everyone has the right and responsibility to use their spiritual gift for the benefit of others.

Whether it is the Catholic mass, the Orthodox liturgy, or the Protestant sermon from the pulpit, it is unfortunately still spectator Christianity. Instead we affirm the apostolic practice of open and participatory meetings: "What then shall we say, brothers? When you come together, *everyone* has a hymn, or a word of instruction, a revelation, a tongue or an interpretation. All of these must be done for the strengthening of the church." (1 Cor 14:26 *NIV*, emphasis added; see also 1 Cor 12:7-12,27-30, 1 Cor 14:36-38, Col 3:16, Eph 5:19-20, Heb 10:25).

The Spirit of God must be allowed to lead and speak *to* the church *through* the church. Jesus should no longer just be the guest of honour in church meetings. He should be the Master of Ceremonies. No more one man shows. No more active few performing for the passive many. No more spectator Christianity.

DECLARATION 8
We Declare Common Homes vs. Holy Buildings

For too long, we Christians have been meeting in sacred structures and 'holy places' such as cathedrals, church buildings, chapels, school gyms, and rented halls. But, the tide is turning! We now declare that grassroots Christianity is best lived out in the context of ordinary, everyday, 'common' homes as a living room movement.

Certainly, special church buildings are not evil or wrong in themselves, but their serious limitations should cause us to reconsider their use. First, church buildings breed a 'temple mentality' that creates a spectator experience of church. Second, it prevents Christians from permeating into their very neighbourhoods and workplaces with the gospel of peace. Third, the massive practical release of time, energy, and money from the elimination of building projects and/or rental payments would free up resources toward caring for the poor and supporting mobile apostolic workers who start new communities of faith in unreached areas.

Homes and house-sized churches in comparison are natural, simple, inexpensive, adaptable, duplicatable, intimate, give everyone a chance to fully participate during meetings, and are a natural breeding ground for leadership development. It is no wonder that the first century church, many subsequent reform, renewal, and revival movements, and the most rapid church planting movements today primarily utilize multiplying house-sized groups (Acts 12:12, 16:14-15,29-34, 20:20; Rom 16:3-5; 1 Cor 16:19; Col 4:15; Philem 1:2).

DECLARATION 9
We Declare Common Days vs. Holy Days

For too long, we Christians have been attached to liturgical calendars, sabbaths, commemorations, and other 'holy days' like Sunday. But, the tide is turning! We now declare that grassroots Christianity is to be lived out every day of the year, at all times, in all seasons.

Christians are free to meet at all times and be the church 24 hours a day, 7 days a week, 365 days a year, rather than feeling superstitiously duty bound to observe certain days. We agree with the apostle Paul: "Formerly, when you did not know God, you were slaves to those who by nature are not gods. But now that you know God—or rather are known by God—how is it that you are turning back to those weak and miserable principles? Do you wish to be enslaved by them all over again? You are observing special days and months and seasons and years! I fear for you, that somehow I have wasted my efforts on you." (Gal 4:8-11 *NIV;* see also Rom 14:4-6, Col 2:16-17).

Therefore, we are free to meet, encourage one another, and reach out to the world at all times and everyday.

DECLARATION 10

We Declare Common Goods vs. Holy Fees

For too long, we Christians have supported church systems through compulsory financial giving of members. But, the tide is turning! We now declare that grassroots Christians are to give voluntarily and cheerfully based on their ability and the need of the moment.

The traditional approach to financial matters stands in stark contrast to the patterns we see in the New Testament (Acts 2:43-45, 4:32-35, 11:27-30, Rom 15:25-28, 1 Cor 16:1-4, 2 Cor 9:1-15, Gal 2:1,9-10).

First, much of the financial giving in traditional churches has by necessity gone towards building mortgages and rental payments, local clergy and staff salaries, and expensive programs and services. However, the first century church was free of such elements and collected money primarily in support of two groups of people when they had need. This included the poor among them and mobile apostolic workers who started new churches or traveled widely to encourage existing ones. Local house church elders, though, were volunteers. In this way they lived a shared life together and gave to each other as they had need.

Second, much traditional giving has in effect been a church tax to support the 'cathedral' church system, usually in the form of the 10% tithe. This, however, is nowhere encouraged in the New Testament as a normative binding practice for Christians. Instead, the apostolic principle taught was one of generosity. Everyone gave when and how much they could to whoever needed help, cheerfully and voluntarily, and never under compulsion or by guilt.

Therefore, we advocate a return to New Testament principles and practices concerning money and resources.

Grassroots Christians of All Nations, Unite !!!

QUESTIONS FOR GROUP REFLECTION

1. *Declarations.* Which of the 10 declarations listed really resonates with you? Which one concerns you?

2. *Renewal, Reform, and Revival.* What do you make of the statement that 'The history of the Christian Church is simply the story of the struggle between prophetic and institutional religion'? How does this apply today?

GROUP EXERCISE

Get together and watch a movie or clip from the life of a Christian or Christian movement that tried to steer the church back to some long lost teaching or practice of the early church. You may consider renting a video from a Christian bookstore on Martin Luther, George Fox, John Wesley, the Anabaptists, etc.

6

PRACTICAL CONSIDERATIONS
GETTING HOUSE CHURCHES
GOING AND GROWING

Because New Testament-style house church gatherings are still a fledgling phenomenon in many places, there are uncertainties and practical questions that need to be addressed. This chapter provides practical advice in getting your house church going and growing (Please see *Appendix 3* for the "Top 10 Reasons for Starting House Churches"). The following is based on the author's experiences in starting and leading small groups and house churches, the patterns established by the apostles for the church, a study of church history and missions, prayer and reflection, and interactions with others in the house church movement. Just as any living organism goes through successive stages of development, so too might a house church. The discussion below examines the following five key stages: (1) starting, (2) functioning, (3) growing, (4) birthing, and (5) networking.

1. STARTING A HOUSE CHURCH

Establish a Clear Vision

It is vitally important to blueprint from the outset both the purpose and structure of the house church. There must be a radical commitment to the Bible as being the ultimate authority for church practice. A biblical house church is one that is, first and foremost, a gathering of believers around Christ in which there is an open, participatory, and interactive use of everyone's spiritual gifts for mutual benefit.[207] This is not about simply transplanting a traditional Sunday morning church service into someone's living room, with an active few performing for the passive many. Nor is a house church simply an add-on to a traditional congregation, as is the case for prayer groups, Bible study groups, and cell groups. To recap, New Testament-style house churches are fully functioning churches in and of themselves, with the freedom to partake of the Lord's Supper, baptize, marry, bury, and exercise discipline. They are led by a small team of elders and meet in homes in small groups for prayer, worship, Bible study, discussion, mentoring, outreach, food, and fun. Each house church should be linked together with others into a cohesive network for stability, accountability, and vision. A firm commitment to and understanding of this is necessary as a healthy starting point, whether the initial group is composed of long-time Christians or spiritual newborns.

Establish a Core Group

Find others who feel strongly called by God to move in this direction. This initial group will likely form the core team out of which God will begin to build a network of house churches. So, it is important that the folks who make up this core group evidence a clear sense of call, understanding, and commitment to the endeavor. Although we must allow for the fact that there will always be a mixture of pioneers, early adopters, late adopters, and laggards in any Christian community, it is wise to be very selective as to who makes up this initial cluster.

Many Christians, however well meaning, may actually thwart the new house church by bringing distracting ideas into the mix or may want to join in simply because of the excitement of being part of something new. Just as Jesus did not choose his twelve disciples haphazardly but did so through a great deal of reflection, prayer, and interaction, we also do not need to fear being very selective at the start.[208]

It may also be important to work with an evangelistic or apostolic ministry dedicated to establishing New Testament-style

---

[207] 1 Cor 14:26, Eph 5:19, Col 3:16, Heb 10:24-25
[208] Luke 6:12-16

house churches to get going in these early stages, especially if the initial thrust is evangelistically oriented to establish the core group.

Establish a Target Population

The other important issue for house churches intent on reaching out evangelistically is the target population group. Who is most likely to be attracted to the people already committed to be part of the core team? Will it be a certain racial, linguistic, socio-economic, or age segment of the population? Although in the larger scope of God's economy there is no difference between male and female, rich and poor, educated and uneducated, young and old, or Jew and Gentile,[209] human beings by nature are most often attracted to people like themselves because of familiarity and comfort. This is a fact that was not lost on the apostle Paul in his approach to ministry in being "all things to all men so that by all possible means [he] might save some."[210] Rather than artificially trying to create local heterogeneous groups that try to reflect the diversity of the global body of Christ, the like-attracts-like principle can be accommodated strategically by house church networks. For instance, the most rapid church planting movements today that use house churches and cell groups are happening within ethnic monocultures in places like Latin America, China, India, Cambodia, etc.[211] Thus, those operating in multi-ethnic contexts, in particular, must consider this issue seriously. Once a population segment is discerned, choosing a geographic area or social context for maximum contact with the target group may become the next strategic focus.

2. FUNCTIONING AS A HOUSE CHURCH

Prototyping

It is important to keep in mind that the first house church that is established, as the beginning of a network of house churches, will inevitably become the prototype after which the others are patterned, for better or worse. This will become a test case in which the bugs and problems will need to be resolved, hopefully before the need to multiply into a second house church. So, it is essential to make sure that the initial group is healthy and balanced. The best way to avoid

---

[209] Gal 3:28-29, Col 3:11
[210] 1 Cor 9:19-23 (NIV)
[211] David Garrison, *Church Planting Movements*, 1999.

mistakes and going down dead end streets is to incorporate the core functions found in rapidly growing church planting movements. A balanced diet includes the following five key elements: (i) worship and prayer; (ii) evangelistic and missionary outreach; (iii) education and discipleship; (iv) practical ministry; and (v) fellowship.[212] But, what does this mean practically?

Format

Some Basic Concepts. It must be remembered that the purpose of a biblical house church gathering is not simply to transplant the rigid programmed liturgy of a more traditional Sunday church service into someone's living room. Rather, it is a time where everyone has the opportunity and responsibility of contributing their spiritual gift from God for the benefit of others in the group.

With this in mind, when your home church meets, there are a number of things that you can do as you gather around Christ: prayer, reflection, worship in song, having a meal, discussion Bible study, the Lord's Supper, baptism, free prophecy, etc. These elements can find their way into a meeting either completely spontaneously or in a more planned way.

Whichever way a home church leans, ample opportunity for everyone to participate and contribute is key, as opposed to more traditional Sunday morning meetings in which a chosen few perform for a passive audience. Jesus must be allowed to lead the meeting, rather than simply being the guest of honour.

The role of house church leaders/elders, then, is simply to encourage everyone to participate by throwing out questions and concerns to the group, by prompting shy individuals to participate, and by sensing where the Spirit may want to go next. No one person is to dominate a meeting.

5W Meetings. More specifically, some advocate a structured but flexible format which tries to ensure that key elements are consistently present every meeting to ensure health, balance, and focus, and so that everyone has an opportunity to contribute. They use a flexible 5W format that entails Welcome (ice breaker), Worship (praise and prayer), Word (discussion Bible study), Works (mutual ministry time including prayer, prophecy, or problem-solving), and Witness

---

[212] David Garrison, p.36.

(engaging in, or planning for, an outreach activity). They may then end by breaking into smaller groups in different parts of the house for more concentrated prayer, discussion, and mutual encouragement. In this case, a danger may be that the 5W structure takes on the status of a liturgy or fixed order of service. To prevent this, some home churches alternate between this and a completely open format from meeting-to-meeting to mix things up. This structured format may also simply be a temporary transitional phase until such time that the group gels and understands how to engage in a completely open type of meeting.

Open Meetings. Many house churches practice a completely open type of meeting, in which there is nothing planned at all, but rather everyone brings something to the gathering in keeping with their individual experience of Christ during the past week and/or as Christ leads them to use their 'spiritual gift' during the actual meeting. Everyone individually needs to come ready to share and give to the rest of the group. These are truly Spirit-led meetings as described in 1 Corinthians 12:7-12 and 1 Corinthians 14. There is a releasing of everyone's spiritual gifts and skills.

The first step to developing open meetings may be to relearn and rediscover how to be the church together; this may require that old habits die. Simply beginning your home church by getting together for a meal, without any planned agenda for prayer or Bible study or anything we think we know about church, may be a good start. Just come prepared to share and participate. Then, as your group gets together over a period of time around a meal, you will discover by Christ's leading what to *do* and how to *be* the church to one another. The only thing that people need to do is come prepared to share and participate. This is somewhat like using the Last Supper—with Jesus and his twelve disciples gathered around a full meal discussing the things of God—as a model for how a house church can meet.

Organization

Regarding organizational details, there are several pragmatic issues that need to be considered.

Frequency. It is recommended that a home church meet one to three times per week to maintain a sense of connectedness with one another. Meeting less frequently than this will tend to kill momentum. Meeting more frequently may simply lead to burnout, especially for those expected to facilitate something regularly.

When to Meet. Of course, choosing a time that is convenient for everyone involved seems to be an obvious choice. However, the reader should also consider meeting on Sunday mornings for strategic reasons in particular. This will force current and future participants to choose whether they are truly part of the house church, or whether it is simply supplemental to their involvement with a more traditional church in town. This will filter out those people who are just looking for the next new fad on the Christian landscape and who never really plan on committing to the house church as their primary community.

Length. It is typical that meeting times last between one-and-a-half to three hours to allow for adequate depth and participation from everyone. There should also be a clear ending time to the gathering (unless the Spirit says otherwise) so that those who need to leave can do so without guilt and without missing anything important. Others, of course, are free to continue on.

Place. Choosing a home to meet in can work in two ways. Some choose to meet in the same home for consistency's sake, because of the size and comfort of the particular home, or because of the obvious knack for hospitality that the hosts have. Others, on the other hand, choose to have a rotating schedule so that everyone has a chance to host and take on an increased level of ownership for the house church and to avoid overburdening the same host home.

Size. Because home churches value an open, participatory, and family atmosphere as opposed to an organizational one, it is wise to keep the number of people to, say, between 6 and 12. From the author's experience, groups less than 6 strong tend to dwindle and be lackluster because of the decreased number of relationships and interactions possible. However, groups over 12 tend to lose intimacy and every-member participation. It is perhaps not surprising, then, that rapid church planting movements today reproduce small house churches and/or cell groups numbering between 10 and 30 people.[213]

Type. The vast majority of home churches today are single-cell creatures, meaning that there is one main group time in which

---

[213] David Garrison, p.35.

everyone participates. These house churches try to maintain intimacy by keeping a small group dynamic deliberately. Others, however, utilize multi-cell setups. This may look like, say, a large group of 20 to 30 people gathering for the first part of the meeting in the largest room in the house, followed by smaller break out groups in the various other rooms for more up-close-and-personal interaction. Still others have several 'cell groups' meeting weekly, with all the cells getting together in someone's home monthly for 'house church'.

Children. One of the first questions that usually come up when talking with people considering house church is the role of children. Three approaches commonly used are integration, specialization, and parental apprenticeship.

By integration it is meant that some house churches try to incorporate teens and children fully into the meetings, making sure that their needs are met and that they have the opportunity to contribute to the gatherings. These groups value a truly multi-generational approach where younger generations are also given the chance to teach the older ones something.

By specialization it is meant that some have a separate time for the young kids in another part of the home that is focused on meeting them where they're at. It may be that a group of home churches will band together to have some sort of specialized occasional programming for children and teens. In the case of older teens or those going about to step into college or university, a house church may be completely comprised of and led by young people, with the support and accountability of the house church network they belong to.

The parental apprenticeship approach is one that places the responsibility of spiritual guidance mainly on the parents during their daily routine dealings with their children. For better or worse, it is often mom and dad that have the biggest influence on a young person's life because of the time spent with them. Children and young teens tend to imitate what they see in their parents, making this a challenge to moms and dads to really live out the Christian life in front of their kids. Becoming overly dependent on specialized programming does not acknowledge this fact and detracts from the opportunity and responsibility of Christian parents to raise their children in the things of the Lord as they go about the day-to-day activities of family life.[214] Although specialized programming for young children and teens has merit, it should be a supplement to parental mentoring rather than a substitute for it.

Community Life

House church is not only about a series of meetings that happen weekly in someone's home. A key ingredient is building spiritually transforming relationships in the context of the ebb and flow of daily life and ministry. For the sake of accountability, encouragement, mentoring, and leadership development, the 'meetings between meetings' on informal and planned levels are vital. A home church is meant to be a family, a 24-hour-a-day, 7-day-a-week community, which is the crucible that God uses to see change take place in our lives. So, what does this mean practically? It means both quality and quantity time with each other.[215] This is about mutual life-on-life ministry and about giving each other permission to enter into each other's lives. We should not underestimate the power of spending time together walking, eating, shopping, playing sports, mowing the lawn, watching a movie, going for a coffee, etc. In these informal times, it has been said that more is caught than is formally taught. Robert Coleman, in his classic book *The Master Plan of Evangelism*, makes the following astute observation about how Jesus informally trained his twelve disciples and built a sense of group identity among them:

> The time which Jesus invested in these few disciples was so much more by comparison to that given to others that it can only be regarded as a deliberate strategy. He actually spent more time with his disciples than with everybody else in the world put together. He ate with them, slept with them, and talked with them for the most part of his entire active ministry. They walked together along the lonely roads; they visited together in the crowded cities; they sailed and fished together on the Sea of Galilee; they prayed together in the deserts and in the mountains; and

---

[214] Deut 11:19, Prov 22:6

[215] Jean Vanier, *Community and Growth*, Paulist Press, 1989; Dietrich Bonhoeffer, *Life Together*, Harper and Row, 1954.

they worshiped together in the synagogues and in the Temple.[216]

One-to-One Discipleship Chains

As described earlier in Chapter 2, I have had three men who have been significant spiritual fathers to me. Through these men, I can directly trace my spiritual heritage back seven generations to Dawson Trotman, founder of the Christian missions organization *The Navigators*. Now, I didn't know Dawson Trotman and he didn't know me, but because of his willingness sixty years ago to be available to God and invest his energy into a few individuals, my life has been deeply impacted. Tens of thousands around the world today are able to say the same thing.

This practice of taking an individual under your wing is a thoroughly biblical one. In the New Testament we see Barnabas encouraging Paul in the early days of his faith, Paul deeply influencing Timothy to step up into leadership, and then Timothy training the next generation of leaders. Earlier in the Old Testament we notice Elijah spiritually fathering Elisha, David and Jonathan having a peer mentoring relationship going on, Moses preparing Joshua for leadership, etc. Biblical leadership training and discipleship was most often done using a hands-on, on-the-job, apprenticeship approach.

Consequently, it is paramount in this writer's view and experience that intentional one-on-one discipleship and a 'discipleship chain' vision be an integral part of the house church movement.[217]

Who needs a spiritual coach? Everyone. People needing discipleship include those on the threshold of faith, new Christians, growing Christians, people going through a personal crisis, but also emerging and current leaders. In other words, there is no point in our journey with Christ that we cannot benefit from someone else who is farther down the road. Although there are many teachers in the body

---

[216] Robert Coleman, *The Master Plan of Evangelism*, Revell, 1994, p.45.

[217] Larry Kreider, *The Cry for Spiritual Fathers and Mothers*, House to House Publications, 2000; Jim Peterson, *Lifestyle Discipleship*, NavPress, 1993; Paul Stanley and Robert Clinton, *Connecting: The Mentoring Relationships You Need to Succeed*, NavPress, 1992.

of Christ, there is a lack of, but deep need for, spiritual fathers and mothers who journey alongside people to see them grow.

Who is qualified to be a mentor? Anyone. As long as we are willing for God to use us to help someone else move forward spiritually, passing on to them what we know, we are qualified. This does not mean that we will have all the answers or be able to take someone as far as they need, but we are certainly able to help those we are slightly ahead of to take a few more steps forward.

What approach should be used? One that works for both the mentor and the mentored. My personal experience in receiving and giving mentorship has been intentional weekly one-on-one meetings over several months and in some cases years, in which life issues, spiritual questions, and ministry skill development are addressed. This, of course, is in combination with informal interactions during the ebb and flow of daily life and ministry. Actually ministering together can be a very powerful experience. You may decide to visit a sick friend in the hospital together, go for a prayer walk around the city, witness together to a mutual friend, etc. Others prefer a much more casual approach, which includes many informal social times that create a context for deeper conversations. Discipleship happens best when it happens 'life-on-life'.

What about expectations and boundaries? The specific areas of need should be identified by both people involved in the mentoring relationship and may include marriage, finances, family, sexuality, culture, career, academics, and ministry vision and skill. Boundaries that can be created right at the start include the frequency and length of the meeting times, the duration of the mentoring relationship, the degree of deliberateness, and any life circumstances that could bring an end to the process. This may be particularly needed when coaching very 'high needs' individuals. And, only same-gender mentoring is recommended, unless unusual circumstances exist or there are extremely clear safeguards, because of the potential danger of a mentoring bond developing into an inappropriate romantic one.

What results should we expect to see? It is important to model things as much as it is to teach because this is about life-on-life ministry. Consequently, we will reproduce after our own 'kind', whether we like it or not. If we are weak in prayer, then it may not come as a surprise that the person we're helping along will develop the same habits. If we are strong in one area, such as evangelism, then it's likely they will develop the same spiritual muscles. I am not implying here that the person we are coaching has no mind or personality or talents of their own and that they will simply mimic what they see in us. This may not be the case for growing or mature believers, but it may be the case when apprenticing new Christians.

In the end, if we take to heart this challenge of spiritually linking the generations by a deliberate discipleship process, we will be poised to establish a spiritual heritage that will multiply and reproduce itself into a mighty army of God.

The Role of House Church Leaders

Although key characteristics of house churches are their open, interactive, and participative nature, there is still a practical need for some form of leadership to bring health and growth. As far as possible, it is best to have a small team of two or three people in each house church that will act as the leaders (called 'elders' in the New Testament) with the dual responsibilities of shepherding and strategizing. The following also applies in general terms to mobile apostolic leaders, except on a broader scale and as it pertains to their larger scope of responsibility and activity.

Shepherd. This refers to the nurturing 'heart' aspect of eldership.[218] The shepherding function of an elder is to set the tone for the group regarding atmosphere and emotional safety. An elder will also stimulate relationships between people, resolve conflicts, pray for people, and be aware of people's particular interests and growth needs. This does not mean that elders are solely responsible for the nurture of everyone in the group by acting as everyone's personal chaplain. Nor are they the only ones in a home church that have pastoring/shepherding gifts. Rather, it simply means that they ensure that everyone's needs are being met in some way, whether by them, someone else, or something else. This requires awareness on their part. An elder should also be responsible for ensuring that the Lord's Supper and baptism are carried out appropriately, although they may not necessarily be physically administering the activity.

---

[218] Henri Nouwen, *In the Name of Jesus: Reflections of Christian Leadership*, Crossroad, 1998.

Strategist. This describes the decision-making 'head' aspect of eldership.[219] The strategizing function of an elder is to organize the group, identify and train emerging elders, model and encourage evangelism, and lead out in multiplying or planting other house churches. This does not mean that elders are to be the dictators of the group, making decisions without consulting everyone else. Rather, they are to communicate and model the bigger vision of multiplying house churches, evangelism, and discipleship, and mobilize the house church as a team to accomplish this.

The Training of House Church Leaders

For house churches to be healthy, growing, and multiplying, leaders must be trained adequately to be good shepherds and strategists. The vision statement of *House Church Canada*, which I co-founded with Jason Johnston, is both challenging and exciting: *"Train Leaders to Multiply House Churches that Reach the Nations for Christ."* To accomplish this, some combination of three training processes are strongly recommended for local and mobile leaders, namely the leaders huddle, the apprenticeship approach, and formal training.

The Leaders Huddle. This involves the leaders of a house church or a network of house churches getting together once or twice monthly for intentional leadership development. This can be called the '4D' approach, which stands for Dream-Drill-Discuss-Dinner. 'Dream' involves a teaching that clearly communicates the larger vision or purpose of your house church network. 'Drill' attempts to address practical hands-on nuts-and-bolts issues that will be faced by house church leaders, like leading effective group discussions, mentoring people, evangelism strategies, etc. 'Discuss' may include a time of open group conversation, Q & A, or group brainstorming about current problems. 'Dinner' caps things off nicely and gives people a chance to unwind and interact casually.

Apprenticeship. This approach utilizes the M.A.W.L. principle, which stands for Model, Assist, Watch, and Leave. This has been used successfully in one church planting movement in a remote region of China that grew from three churches in 1993 to 550 churches by 1998.[220] 'Model' refers to the act of being a first

---

[219] Robert Coleman, *The Master Plan of Evangelism*, 1994.
[220] David Garrison, pages 19 and 44.

generation house church, which includes the emerging leaders who will eventually lead a second generation of house churches. 'Assist' involves helping this first house church to multiply or plant another one, with the new leaders taking on its leadership. 'Watch' is the process of ensuring that the second-generation house church starts a third generation house church without any direct involvement from the original house church or its leaders. 'Leave' refers to fully releasing the second and third generation house churches to be self-sustaining. This creates a 'multiplying and planting' mentality among all the house churches in a network. The M.A.W.L. principle can be applied as one house church spawns a second generation house church or as an individual discipler coaches their disciple into a discovery of their calling and full use of their spiritual gifts.

Formal Training. This route refers to the importance of having a few individuals with theological training from a seminary or Bible college floating around the house church movement to ensure its theological health. These folks can provide some of the necessary academic tools to ensure both theological breadth and depth. This is not to say that every single house church or even network needs to have someone like this but, conversely, it will not do to have a dynamic movement that is going off the rails on some key doctrinal points. Even so, the capability of so-called lay people to become self-taught and very knowledgeable, perhaps by even taking a few courses or extensive personal reading and study, should not be underestimated.

Without being deliberate about all or some of the above approaches, the quality and quantity of emerging leaders can be severely compromised.

The Financial Support of House Church Leaders

One of the main thrusts within the house church movement is a return to the simplicity of first century apostolic patterns. So, the subject of financial support of the two primary types of New Testament leadership—local and mobile—is also to be addressed from a biblical standpoint as described in Chapter 3, 'Church, First Century Style'.

Local Leaders. Citywide house church elders were those who had the character and competence to effectively manage the affairs of the church in their locality. Their mandate was long-term and local, functioning as both lead shepherds and strategists for the citywide church. Ideally, a small team of elders would have also managed each house church. However, in contrast to much post-biblical church tradition and contemporary practice, they were not professional clergy who received regular salaried financial support. Rather, they were volunteers who had jobs like everyone else and so could relate to the ups-and-downs of working life experienced by others.

Traveling from group to group in the first century, one would have been immediately struck by the non-professional nature of church leadership. This created an atmosphere where everyone could potentially become a leader. It was a volunteer "lay" movement that effectively maximized on everyone's spiritual contribution and, hence, was a breeding ground for leaders. Because house churches were small in size (less than 30 members), a small team of two or three volunteer elders easily provided adequate leadership. As such, it is recommended that today's emerging house church movement maintain the "lay", unpaid, non-professional status of local leadership.

Mobile Leaders. The counterparts to local leaders in the first century were the traveling apostolic workers whose mandate was temporary and universal. Their job was typically to go to unreached regions to establish new churches by evangelizing the populace, baptizing new converts, organizing believers into local house churches, and appointing local citywide elders. They would also circulate from group-to-group and city-to-city to provide ongoing personal coaching. Because they could not be tied down to local jobs, they required some sort of ongoing financial support for their work. In most cases they gladly received such financial assistance, e.g. Peter, whereas in other cases they were financially independent because of the transportable nature of their trade, e.g. the apostle Paul and his tent-making career.[221]

Interestingly, the house church movement in China has made a deliberate decision to only give monetary aid to traveling evangelists and church planters who start churches in new untapped areas, while local house church leaders remain volunteers.[222] This focuses their

---

[221] 1 Cor 9:1-18
[222] Larry Kreider, *House Church Networks*, pp.41-42.

resources on going into the world and making disciples of all nations, rather than pouring money into buildings and expensive programs.

So, in this light, it is suggested that today's emerging movement attempt to provide financial support primarily to 'apostolic' workers, namely those coaching citywide or regional house church networks and those who have a calling to make a geographic move to begin house church networks from ground zero in new areas.

3. GROWING A HOUSE CHURCH

Put simply, there are two primary ways to grow a house church, namely by having Christians join or by leading people to Christ. Both of these avenues have their own challenges and opportunities.

Reaching out to Christians

A house church may decide to seek out those Christians who are currently on the fringe of traditional churches, are church dropouts, are looking for a new church, or are looking for a house church in particular. My current house church has had a number of inquiries and visitors from the entire spectrum, who have heard by word of mouth or from our website. For many, house church is simply a curiosity or the latest new fad, whereas others have been genuinely interested. One of the challenges of having Christians join your house church is that the paradigm of 'church' that exists in people's minds (i.e. Sunday services, a building, a full time pastor, etc.) is hard to change. Some may eventually start asking when the house church will be getting a full time pastor, or when the youth group will begin, or when the building program will start. Thus, the vision of house church must be communicated very clearly from the outset. The advantage, however, of having Christians join is that there is a level of spiritual maturity already present, as well as their friendship circles, that can be drawn upon to grow the house church.

Reaching out to Non-Christians

Seeking out those who don't know Christ is the other way of growing house churches. Both individual and group efforts should be made consistently over the long haul for real fruit to emerge.

Individual Evangelism. House churches should train members to effectively and naturally share their faith with friends, family, neighbours, and coworkers.[223] Some tips are: identify and focus on your sphere of influence; spend quantity and quality time with non-Christians; reach out in practical ways; learn the art of asking questions; learn to share your story of faith using plain everyday language; become informed about Biblical reliability issues and world religions. Other individuals may be particularly talented at public speaking or more cold contact methods and may seek out a context in which this can be done, such as giving a seminar on some aspect of Christian faith or life at the local library or campus lecture hall, street or open-air preaching, going door-to-door, etc. Some of the latter methods, though, may not particularly work well in Western society, which values its privacy and avoids confrontation.

Group Evangelism. Each house church should embrace its immediate neighbourhood as its primary arena of outreach. The key to this is to keep all efforts as relational, natural, creative, practical, and intentional as possible. There are a number of resources available that offer practical ways a house church can reach out as a team to friends, acquaintances, and neighbours.[224] One of the pluses of reaching out as a group is that everyone becomes involved, instead of just a few individuals who may be more gifted evangelistically. Some ideas include: have monthly dinner parties; organize a neighbourhood block party or BBQ; get involved in a community project; organize a neighbourhood food drive for the local food bank; get involved in the local soup kitchen or homeless shelter; host an introductory Bible study or an *Alpha Course*[225] discussion dinner group; set up an information booth at the mall; organize a coffee house in a pub, restaurant, or community centre; have a public showing of the Jesus film or a mainstream movie; get involved with a mass-evangelism ministry in following up on new believers, etc.

---

[223] Michael Green, *One to One: How to Share your Faith with a Friend*, Moorings, 1995; Jim Peterson, *Living Proof*, NavPress, 1989; Rebecca Pippert, *Out of the Saltshaker and into the World*, InterVarsity Press, 1999.
[224] Joel Comiskey, *Home Cell Group Explosion*, Touch Publications, 1999.
[225] *The Alpha Course* is a lively 15-part video series that introduces the Christian faith and is accompanied by a number of resources including the book *Questions of Life: A Practical Introduction to the Christian Faith* (Nicky Gumbel, Cook Ministry Resources, 1996).

4. BIRTHING NEW HOUSE CHURCHES

There are two approaches that are typically used in starting new house churches, namely multiplying and planting. Both of these possibilities should be communicated on a regular basis as an inherent value and goal of the house church. Our house church network has adopted the slogan, *"Every Church, Start a Church, Every Year"*. To multiply or plant a new house church of 10 people each year is not an unreasonable goal. Doing the math, a 10-year commitment to this process could produce as many as 1000 house churches. Ultimately, the vision would be to implement a saturation strategy by establishing a house church on every city block or in a given geographic zone across a city.

Multiplying New Groups

This refers to the numerical growth of a house church to the point where there is a need to split the group into two to start a second group. House churches typically undergo this process every 6 to 18 months. When should a house church multiply? The answer depends on whether the house church wants to replicate a single-cell or multi-cell pattern.

Single-cell house churches try to maintain the intimacy of being a single small group. In this case, the group begins preparing to multiply at about 20 people or so, since the family dynamic and closeness will begin to wane. How should such a house church multiply? We recommend this be done in stages because of the relationship separation anxiety that is usually involved. There may be an initial acclimatization stage where, say, all 20 people gather in the same home, have a large group time, and then break out into two groups of 10 into different rooms in the house. This multi-cell arrangement may last temporarily for a short duration of, say, several months with a deadline date for final multiplication into a second home.

Multi-cell house churches, on the other hand, simultaneously combine the excitement of a large group dynamic with the intimacy of small groups. Gathering times may look like a large group gathering time of 20-30 folks followed by smaller break out groups for more up-close-and-personal mutual ministry. This pattern is maintained deliberately in the long-term. Hiving off into a second house church may not occur until the group approaches 40 people.

Planting New Groups

This refers to a house church taking on the challenge of sending out a small 'apostolic' team to start a new house church in another area of town. This new core team may be drawing on an existing relational network or starting from scratch, as described earlier in the section 'Starting a House Church'.

One scenario may be that the team starts by using their own home as a spiritual beachhead for hosting an introductory Bible study or the *Alpha Course* with non-Christian friends and acquaintances. As people come to Christ in due course, will transition into a house church by gradually adding more intensive elements such as prayer, the Lord's Supper, worship, open meetings, etc.

Another arrangement uses the 'person of peace' principle. The planting team seeks out an individual who is responsive to the message of Christ and is willing to open up their own home to have their friends over for a seeker-driven Bible study. Under the direction of the team, this Bible study then begins a process of shifting more towards a full-fledged house church. There are several case studies in the Scriptures of planting house churches using this strategy,[226] which is being used successfully today in both China and India.[227]

5. NETWORKING HOUSE CHURCHES

Individual cells in a body cannot go it alone for long and will eventually die without being interconnected with other cells. It is absolutely crucial that house churches form networks that pray, plan, and play together.[228] So long as house churches choose isolation, independence, and inwardness, so long will they remain a mere novelty, a trend, a fad, without ever becoming a real movement that deeply impacts their city, region, or nation with the gospel of Christ. They must unite! There are five reasons for linking house churches together rather than promoting isolated and independent groups:

---

[226] Luke 10:1-11; Acts 10:1-48, 16:13-18

[227] Friday Fax, "China: Are Women the More Effective Evangelists?", Issue 13, March 29, 2002, fridayfax@bufton.net; Friday Fax, "Thousands of Hindus find Jesus in Houses of Prayer", Issue 31, August 2, 2002, fridayfax@bufton.net

[228] Peter Bunton's study of church history in *Cell Groups and House Churches* (2001) clearly shows that movements that were vibrant made a conscious effort to link together their cells and/or house churches.

Biblical Example. The early church functioned on a regional or citywide level as a cohesive unit to reach out to their communities because of the 'theology of unity'—the oneness of the body of Christ—that they embraced.

Human Psychology. There is a deep human need to belong to something greater than a small local house church. It's exciting to know that we are part of something global and that we are part of God's plan for not only our neighbourhood, but also the world.

Social Needs. Individual and isolated house churches tend to be very ingrown and have difficulty in meeting all the social needs of its members (e.g. single people desiring to get married, teens looking for friends, children in search of playmates, etc.). A collection of groups can bridge the gap in these areas.

Teamwork Pays Off. The combined efforts and skills of a web of house churches working together can propel it to movement status, something that an equal number of isolated house churches will have much more difficulty accomplishing because of their lack of vision and resources and their tendency to scatter.

Integrity in Doctrine and Behaviour. Independent groups may be precursors to cults and sects. There is no point in multiplying a vast array of independent house churches that are teaching heresy, that become personality cults, or that are treating people badly. A web of churches can make sure that the core teachings of Christ and the apostles are honoured and applied in a healthy way.

Therefore, as more home churches emerge, they will need to become part of house church networks if the citywide unity of the body of Christ is to be valued, if momentum is to increase on local, regional, and national levels, and if health and stability is to be maintained. There are three levels of networking that can take place, namely local, regional, and national. Please refer to *Appendix 2 – The Early Church as an Organized Movement* as the model for how house church networks can function biblically and effectively today.

Local Networks

A local, or citywide, network is a close-knit family of house churches because of the deliberateness, frequency, and intensity of interaction between them. These working partnerships transcend any official denominational ties that house churches might have. This can happen in five concrete ways.

Large Public Meetings. All the house churches can gather together, say, monthly for a time of worship, teaching, testimony, food, and fun in a rented space somewhere, outdoors, or in a very large home. This is meant to be a community gathering time, an extended family reunion, which reflects the personality of that family. However, these large group settings can also be used as evangelistic opportunities rather than as 'worship' or 'celebration' services for believers. Those coming to faith or desiring to investigate further can be directed to a house church near them. These large occasional public meetings, though, should only function as 'icing on the cake' and should never rival the dominant practice of house-to-house meetings.

House-to-House Visits. House churches can visit each other on a scheduled rotating basis or informally. This allows for more up-close-and-personal relationships and accountability to develop and an enhanced sense of belonging to something greater than one's own house church.

Leaders Huddles. Regular leadership meetings bring the elders of home groups together to pray, exchange resources, strategize, train, encourage, and keep each other accountable. A small apostolic team that coaches the network can pull this together. Or, local elders can be designated as facilitators on a rotating basis so that every elder has a chance to develop their own leadership abilities further. Our network currently does this every month and finds it vital.

Mobile Circuit Riders. A few called individuals of character and competence can move from group-to-group (or city-to-city in the case of regional networks) like the first-century apostles or the early Methodist circuit riders. They may act as the apostolic workers who coach the home church web on a routine basis by providing consultation, encouragement, as well as reminding the local groups about the big picture. However, it is healthiest if these folks are also involved in their own local house church. The house church network in their care should consider financially giving to these apostolic workers as the Lord leads. This requires partnership and trust between local and mobile leaders.

Networks of Networks. If a network becomes too large, then multiplying into several relatively independent networks may be the solution. For instance, if a grouping comprises, say, thirty house churches, this may lead to difficulties in coordination and partnership. This large network, thus, can hive off into three clusters of ten house churches each. Each of these groupings will then have their own eldership team and an apostolic coach and will relate with other networks relationally in a horizontal way. This will help keep a horizontal multiplying mentality alive (which is the biblical pattern), rather than the vertical pyramid leadership structures often seen in today's institutional churches.

Regional Networks

A multi-city network may function more like an informal friendship between house church groupings within a given state or province. The frequency and interaction will be similar to, but less involved than, local groupings. There may be annual gatherings of all home churches together in a coliseum or arena for celebration, teaching, and testimony. In addition, house church leadership may gather several times each year for prayer, encouragement, brainstorming, planning, and resource exchange. Conferences and workshops may be organized that specifically address the needs of the region. There may even be an apostolic leadership team that coaches and ignites the regional movement, moving from city-to-city like the apostles of old or the early Methodist circuit riders.

National Networks

Countrywide networking and communication can be fostered through the internet, various publications, and annual strategic consultations. For example, the Canadian House Church Resource Network[229] is attempting to bring countrywide awareness and connection by publishing a newsletter, organizing regional and national consultation groups, and advertising the tours of well-known house church coaches such as Wolfgang Simson and Robert Fitts.

CONCLUSIONS

This chapter has provided guidelines for starting, functioning, growing, birthing, and linking house churches. You should now have a good idea of what it takes to see a multiplying, sustainable, healthy house church network growing right in your backyard. It's not complicated, but it is hard. Count the cost before you step ahead.

---

[229] Canadian House Church Resource Network,
www.outreach.ca/cpc/housechurches.htm

QUESTIONS FOR GROUP REFLECTION

1. *Starting a House Church.* What is the importance of effectively 'prototyping' the original house church of an emerging house church network?

2. *Functioning as a House Church.* What are the advantages and/or disadvantages of having completely open vs. structured house church meetings?

3. *Growing your House Church.* Which form of evangelism suggested in this chapter are you most comfortable with and gifted in, personal or small group evangelism?

4. *Birthing New House Churches.* What is the difference between planting vs. multiplying new house churches? In your view, is the motto 'every church, start a church, every year' realistic when it comes to house churches?

5. *Networking House Churches.* Why is it vital for house churches to be linked together? What are some practical ways such groupings can function?

GROUP EXERCISE

House Church Multiplication and Discipleship Chains. This exercise works well with a large group of no more than 30. It illustrates the multiplication of house churches and one-on-one discipleship chains. The facilitator (Generation 1) takes a loaf of bread (or bag of jellybeans) and pulls, say, three individuals (Generation 2) aside from the rest of the group (the masses). The loaf (or bag) is divided in three equal portions among the three individuals. They are instructed to eat a small chunk of the bread (or a jellybean) and, in turn, find three other individuals each (Generation 3) and instruct them to do the same. This process continues until the entire group (the masses) has something to eat. By the end of this exercise, it should be clear that a single person investing in a few individuals and teaching them to do the same, is more effective than that same person trying to reach the entire group by themselves.

7

STRATEGIC DIRECTIONS

LAUNCHING HOUSE CHURCH MOVEMENTS

BACKGROUND

This chapter suggests several important steps that can help an emerging house church trend to become a rapidly growing people movement that can disciple nations for Christ. However, typical obstacles sometimes prevent such a thing from happening.

First, there exist many streams and even distortions of biblical house church.[230] There are various groups out there: the glorified Bible study, the post-evangelical, the charismatic (Latter Rain and Word Faith influence), the radical wing (Gene Edwards influence), the fundamentalist, those who use house church merely as a tool for evangelism, the 'us four no more' club, etc. This lack of cohesion is perhaps symptomatic of a lack of direction and vision.

Second, some of these groups tend to be very reactionary and rabidly against the institutional church; they carry a Bible in one hand and a rock in the other. Thus, many house churches are quite independent. Part of this may be due to abuse they have experienced in traditional churches at the hands of controlling leadership. On the other hand, some Christians in conventional churches become defensive when the topic of house church is raised because of

---

[230] Frank Viola, "Some Streams of House Church", www.ptmin.org/streams.htm

ignorance and personal negative encounters with well-meaning but not-so-nice house church folks. These tensions will not help the rest of the Body of Christ get on board with what God seems to be doing through the emerging house churches.

Third, there also do not seem to be any local churches, denominations, or missions groups particularly devoted to starting house churches, although some are starting to make room for it by being involved in such endeavours. This probably comes from a combination of the inertia of traditional ways of doing church, ignorance of what house churches are among most Christians, and/or fear of the reactionary nature of some house churches.

TOWARDS A HOUSE CHURCH MOVEMENT

Given the current climate, it seems that it is more accurate to describe what is going on in North America and the rest of the West as a house church 'trend' (i.e. something that can be observed as happening) rather than as a 'movement' (i.e. something with rapid forward and outward motion). This chapter suggests four strategic steps that may help house church trends in various countries become rapidly growing people movements.

Starting New House Churches

It has been recognized that numerically the most effective way of reaching people for Christ is the genesis of new churches. Church growth guru Peter Wagner, based on his research, has stated that "the single most effective way to evangelize is to plant new churches."[231] But, how is this to be done? The key words to best facilitate this process are: deliberate, rapid, small, saturation, and volunteers.

Deliberate. A conscious effort should be made to plant New Testament-style house churches among unreached people pockets. Why should this be done? The reason is simple: new churches don't just happen. Missiological studies have concluded that church planting movements are customarily preceded by a deliberate strategy to begin new disciple-making communities.[232] An example of this, described earlier in this book, was the formation of 3500

---

[231] Peter Wagner, *Church Planting for a Greater Harvest*, Gospel Light/Regal Books: Ventura, CA, 1990, p.11 (quote used by permission).
[232] David Garrison, *Church Planting Movements*, p.34.

house churches (totaling 70,000 people) in one Indian state in the late 1990s as the result of an intentional planting strategy.[233]

Rapid. House churches need to blueprint themselves with a healthy emphasis on evangelism, the goal being multiplying their house church into two or sending a team to start a new one. Multiplying house churches typically grow large enough to form a second group within 6-9 months.[234] Otherwise, they may eventually stagnate and fold. Our house church network in Toronto has taken on the realistic slogan 'every house church, start a house church, every year'. Doing the math, in ten years there could be as many as 1000 house churches in the region. This is a reasonable goal given that doubling a house church only means going from, say, ten to twenty people over the course of an entire year.

Small. House churches should not grow too large before they decide to multiply. Otherwise, the loss of intimacy, openness, and interaction will eventually compromise the group's attractiveness and plateau the numbers. Currently around the globe, explosive Christian conversion growth from church planting movements is characterized by the reproduction of multiplying house churches and cell groups of no more than 10-30 people.[235] It is known that smaller churches experience a proportionally higher growth rate than larger churches: 1-100 member church (63 % growth in 5 years), 100-200 (23 %), 200-300 (17 %), 300-400 (7 %), and over 1000 (4 %).[236] In other words, churches tend to plateau in numbers as they get larger, making the necessity of continually sending out groups from existing churches to start new ones obvious. Given their mobility, flexibility, simplicity, and low cost, small house churches are the most strategic choice in reaching the masses.

Saturation Focused. Every neighbourhood, apartment complex, work setting, and educational institute should be considered as a potential area for a new house church. Conventional churches are not able to penetrate into many segments of society, necessitating a restructuring and re-strategizing towards a more mobile and flexible

---

[233] James Rutz with Victor Choudhrie, "House Church Explosion in India", House-2-House Magazine, Issue 2, 2002, www.house2house.tv
[234] Wolfgang Simson, p.107.
[235] David Garrison, p.35.
[236] Wolfgang Simson, p.248.

approach that can do the job. Specifically, the idea gaining attention among mission organizations and missiologists is the planting of a church for every 500 to 1000 people so that as many people as possible will have a Christian community nearby.[237]

Volunteer Led. The weight of responsibility and leadership for emerging house church movements should be placed squarely on the shoulders of grassroots volunteers, or so-called lay people. Traditional approaches to church planting and missionary work have always employed, quite literally, the services of the professionally trained. However, current research shows that the extent to which rapid church planting movements are birthed depends on the degree to which indigenous non-professionals are encouraged, trained, and released.[238] Professionals—although having a real role as coaches and strategists and mobile overseers of house church networks—need to give way to a new wave of volunteer Christian leaders from the grassroots.

Conscientiously implementing these ingredients builds momentum in exposing more and more people to Christ in the context of house church as well as developing subsequent generations of leaders.

House Church Networks

As more home churches emerge, they will need to become part of citywide networks if the momentum is to increase further on local, regional, and national levels.

Ways of Linking. The way these networks function practically was addressed in detail in the previous chapter. But, to recap briefly, there are five concrete ways house churches can be interlocked into a tight web: occasional citywide gatherings of all house churches; house-to-house meeting patterns; monthly leadership training of house church leaders; traveling apostolic coaching of a network; and multiplying networks of networks of house churches.

Biblical Reasons. As detailed in Chapter 3, "Church, First-Century Style", we saw that house churches of the first century were not an ocean of little groups scattered across the vast reaches of the

---

[237] Robert Fitts, *The Church in the House*, 2001, pp.55-60.
[238] David Garrison, p.35.

Roman Empire. There were mechanisms that connected them together into a movement that outlived the very empire that soon would seek to contain its growth. The specific strands used to weave the web of this fledgling movement were mobile apostolic workers who brought vision and instruction to the churches, as well as house-to-house meeting patterns and citywide gatherings that brought into reality the truth of the unity of the body of Christ.

Practical Reasons. There are psychological, sociological, synergistic, and doctrinal benefits for developing groupings or clusters of house churches on local, regional, and national levels rather than generating a vast sea of isolated and independent groups. Each of these aspects was detailed in the previous chapter and will not be repeated here.

Concerns of Independent House Churches. To some involved in home churches, this idea is tantamount to heresy because of their strong theological conviction regarding the autonomy of each house church. So, any attempt to build a web of house churches working together, on whatever level, will be viewed with suspicion. For some, another factor may be the hurt experienced at the hands of traditional church leadership that was too controlling. However, as argued both from a pragmatic and biblical perspective, some sort of connectivity needs to be present.

Consequently, those of us called to this work need to use our own common sense and lessons from the practice of the early church by implementing house church networks that will form the fabric for the emergence of full-fledged movements in successive generations.

The Role of Traditional Local Churches

This author proposes that more traditional congregations—which use the 'cathedral' model of a special man performing a special service in a special building—can still have a role in the emergence of house church movements. I am personally aware of traditional churches that have already taken the following steps.

Commissioning House Church Missionaries. Although many in the conventional churches likely will never make the emotional and intellectual paradigm shift to house church networks they can, however, fully release and support those who have made that leap to go out and start them. In other words, conventional churches that are mission minded and want to plant churches should give serious consideration to planting fully functioning and self-sustaining house church networks. This may scare some churches and pastors who don't want to let go of capable people. However, rather than viewing this as a loss, it makes a world of difference if it is seen as a viable missionary endeavor to grow the kingdom. A local congregation may, in fact, choose to adopt the house church planter and financially support them the same way they already buttress more traditional missionaries and para-church workers.

Transitioning to a House Church Network. There are some conventional congregations that will be able to make the transition as an entire community towards selling the building and reorganizing as a house church network. This will free up their resources and time to help the poor, support missions work overseas, help mobile house church planters, and develop local leadership. There are some that have made such a jump.

But, it is unlikely that very traditional churches will make such a shift all at once, if at all. It may require some intermediate steps.

For congregations that really don't have any experience with small groups, this may involve simply beginning to develop a strong small groups ministry over a number of years that primarily involves people already in that church.

For those with a mature small groups ministry, this may involve taking the next step of shifting these small groups towards being evangelistic cell groups, which often can begin to look more and more like house churches.

For those local congregations that are cell-based churches with an equal emphasis on home cell groups and Sunday morning celebrations, the final step may be to drop the building and programs and reorganize as a tight network of house churches.

This shift along the spectrum can be described as occurring from 'church *with* small groups' to 'church *of* small groups' to the more biblical and strategic principle that 'church *is* small groups'.

Each of these steps can move the local Body of Christ into a more functional unity as a citywide church as practiced in the first three centuries.

The Role of Denominations and Missions Groups

Although I believe denominations are in no way God's best for the Body of Christ—rather, the citywide or regional church was the apostolic New Testament pattern—we need to work with what we have at the present time in order to usher in long-term changes. So, the entire people of God need to get behind house churches in one way or another for a movement to really explode in Western nations as they are in most other parts of the world. As mentioned in Chapter 4, there are currently some denominations and missions groups that are supporting house church planting efforts, such as the Southern Baptist Convention, Dove Christian Fellowship International, The Free Methodist Church in Canada, The Foursquare Gospel Church of Canada, and the Navigators of Canada. These organizations are having a role to play in initiating and undergirding house church movements.

Realize. Denominations and missions groups need to understand that New Testament-style house churches have a different DNA from small groups, cell groups, or para-church ministries. They are not appendages of conventional congregations. Rather, they are fully functioning churches in and of themselves that network with others of like mind in their city or region. They do not require nor desire church buildings, expensive programs, professional clergy, or highly choreographed services. Gatherings are open, interactive, and family type meetings around the Lord's Supper as a full meal. They focus on relationships, discipleship, and neighbourhood outreach. All of this will require some redefinition of familiar terms like 'congregation', 'church service', etc.

Release. Organizations that wish to endorse house church efforts from within their own ranks will be faced with the challenge of fully releasing leaders to function according to the DNA built into house church movements. Because house church networks desire to re-establish ancient apostolic patterns and practices for church life, denominations will need to avoid the temptation of trying to force these leaders into long-established traditional roles and categories. Because they are typically at the grassroots, most house church leaders functioning on local and trans-local levels will be so-called lay people. They will need to be given the same freedom as more traditional leaders to function in their calling from God to lead, train, and oversee the next generation of house church leaders.

Reinforce. Established Christian organizations, as already mentioned, are supporting house church efforts by funneling money to aid church planters to get new works off the ground and by offering these leaders resources in the way of seminary-equivalent courses, church planting workshops, training materials, regional leadership networks, etc. This kind of support may accelerate the emergence of house church networks, which might lay dormant in isolated and scattered groups.

Recognize. Denominations and mission agencies also bring recognition and validity to house churches in the eyes of the broader Christian community. This legitimacy, in turn, can open the door for increased openness to future participation by individuals and other denominations not currently involved. Moreover, particularly in North America, the only choice most Christians have is that of the traditional local church. Denominations and missions groups can provide the additional option of house churches to members that have never been completely at home in more traditional settings.

Reform. There may even come a day when some smaller denominations will be prepared to sell all their property and entirely reorganize as regional networks of house churches. They can choose to undergo their own mini reformation back to apostolic practices. The fact that even a single denomination or mission group would be brave enough to do this would be a serious clarion call to others toward a significant reformation in church structure, something many Christian leaders have been seeking and talking about for years. This would mimic what is already going on in other parts of the world with the house church movement.

CONCLUSIONS

This chapter has attempted to outline four strategic steps in seeing the current house church trend become a full-fledged movement, especially in the West, namely by planting house churches, seeing the emergence of house church networks, recognizing the role of conventional congregations, and encouraging efforts by denominations and missions groups. When woven together, the resulting cord can lift us to new heights, from which we will see significant reforms in church structure and rapid accommodation of a massive influx into the Body of Christ.

QUESTIONS FOR GROUP REFLECTION

1. *Starting New House Churches.* Why is it important to deliberately start new house churches as opposed to just growing existing ones?

2. *House Church Networks.* Can you recall the why and how of a functioning web of house churches?

3. *Traditional Christianity.* In your opinion, do conventional churches, denominations, and missions organizations have a role in giving a forward nudge to the house church movement? How realistic is it to expect them to do so? What are the advantages and/or disadvantages of trying to work within traditional structures in starting New Testament style house churches vs. starting from scratch?

4. *Practical Steps.* What practical steps are you able to make at this point in stepping ahead with starting a network of house churches?

GROUP EXERCISE

Get together and watch a documentary covering house church movements occurring around the world today (see 'Recommended Resources' for details on the videos *Against Great Odds* and *Church Planting Movements*).

8

CONCLUSIONS
WHAT NOW?

For many readers, the things discussed in these pages have been revolutionary and, maybe, even disturbing. For others, this book has been the breath of fresh air you've been looking for. For those already involved in the global house church movement, this read may have simply confirmed in broad terms what you're already doing. Wherever you are along this spectrum, my deep desire and passionate prayer has been that all of us will be stimulated to reconsider what the church is really all about and challenged to step out in faith to do something about it. If you've come this far in the book, let me congratulate you.

My purpose has been to recast the lost vision of the church as envisioned and practiced by Jesus and the apostles. Getting back to the simplicity and basics of Christian community, the open and interactive gatherings, the strategically small size, the emphasis on outreach and mentoring, the practice of non-hierarchical leadership, the need for the citywide model of church to emerge, etc., are things that the church—especially in its present form in the West—is in desperate need of recovering. My intention has been to present these issues in a balanced, thorough, persuasive, and kind way.

However, allow me to also add a few strong words of challenge. In comparison to the early Christians, the many grassroots movements throughout history, and what is happening today in places like China, India, and Cuba, the practices of many churches today are not merely adaptations of New Testament principles to new contexts but, rather, they are actually distortions resulting from a pick-and-choose approach. Evangelicals, in particular, take pride in holding fast to the teachings of the apostles. This is evident in doctrinal creeds, local church constitutions, baptismal statements of faith, etc. However, although evangelicals attempt to follow the theological teachings (orthodoxy) of the apostles, they stop short when it comes to *fully* embracing apostolic practices (orthopraxy), i.e. church function and form. Why is this so? Because, out of innocent ignorance at best or apathy at worst, traditions are inherited from the previous generation without passing them under the spotlight of apostolic practice. May we learn from the apostles more readily by embracing their teachings and example for both our faith *and* practice!

What now? Where do you go from here? I would suggest several things, dear reader. Count the cost before you step ahead. Pray long and hard. Talk with those involved in house churches. Really examine the New Testament on these matters. Read church history, particularly about movements that tried to get back to New Testament Christianity like the Lollards, Anabaptists, Quakers, Methodists, etc. Get your hands on other books like this one. Go to conferences on the topic. Visit house churches. Make sure you are in this for the long haul and that God is really calling you into this.

Furthermore, I would discourage anyone from starting or staying on this path because it seems to be trendy, practical, strategic, novel, or happens to meet some personal need or preference. These may be initial reasons for involvement, or just one of the reasons, but they should not be the main reasons in the long run. The core motivation must be that we are convinced that New Testament apostolic patterns are indeed God's blueprint for both the church's function *and* form for all time. Otherwise, next week when circus church, punk rock church, or laser church come to town, we'll be off in a flash to join the next new fad. We must stay rooted in the scriptures, allow the Spirit of God to show us the way, and run with abandon. In this way we will save others and ourselves much heartache and confusion. If enough of us have the courage to go this way, then the resulting reformation of the universal church that follows will better accommodate the great ingathering of people into God's empire in the days to come.

Come quickly, Lord Jesus. Amen.

RECOMMENDED RESOURCES

CHRISTIAN LEADERSHIP AND SPIRITUALITY

- Crabb, Larry (1997), *Connecting: Healing for Ourselves and Our Relationships*, Word Books.
- Nouwen, Henri (1989), *In the Name of Jesus: Reflections on Christian Leadership*, Crossroad.
- Nouwen, Henri (1975), *Reaching Out: The Three Movements of the Spiritual Life*, Doubleday.
- Sanders, Oswald (1989), *Spiritual Leadership*, Moody Press.
- Whitney, D.S. (1991), *Spiritual Disciplines for the Christian Life*, NavPress.
- Willard, Dallas (1988), *The Spirit of the Disciplines*, Harper and Row.
- Wilkes, C.G. (1998), *Jesus on Leadership*, Tyndale House.

MENTORING AND DISCIPLESHIP

- Albom, M. (1997), *Tuesdays with Morrie*, Doubleday.
- Bruce, A.B. (1988), *The Training of the Twelve*, Kregel Publications.
- Coleman, Robert (1993), *The Master Plan of Evangelism*, Spire.
- Eims, Leroy (1978), *The Lost Art of Disciple Making*, Zondervan.
- Henrichsen, W. (1988), *Disciples are Made Not Born*, Chariot Victor Books.
- Kreider, Larry (2000), *The Cry for Spiritual Fathers and Mothers*, House to House Publications.
- Petersen, Jim (1993), *Lifestyle Discipleship*, NavPress.
- Sanny, Lorne, *Making the Investment of Your Life*, (4 audio cassettes), NavPress.
- Stanley, P.D. and J.R. Clinton (1992), *Connecting: The Mentoring Relationships You Need to Succeed*, NavPress.

EVANGELISM AND APOLOGETICS

- Barnett, P.B. (1986), *Is the New Testament Reliable?* InterVarsity Press.

- Bruce, F.F. (1992), *The New Testament Documents: Are they Reliable?* InterVarsity Press.
- Green, M. and A. McGrath (1995), *How Shall We Reach Them?* Thomas Nelson Publishers.
- Green, M. (1995), *One to One: How to Share your faith with a Friend,* Moorings.
- Hunter, G.G. (2000), *The Celtic Way of Evangelism.* Abingdon Press.
- Jacks, B. et al (1987), *Your Home a Lighthouse: Hosting an Evangelistic Bible Study,* NavPress.
- Little, P. (1989), *Know Why You Believe,* InterVarsity Press.
- Petersen, Jim (1989), *Living Proof: Sharing the Gospel Naturally,* NavPress.
- Pippert, Rebecca (1999), *Out of the Saltshaker and into the World,* InterVarsity Press.
- Sjogren, S. (1993), *The Conspiracy of Kindness: A Refreshing New Approach of Sharing the Love of Jesus with Others,* Vine Books.
- Strobel, Lee (1998), *The Case for Christ,* Zondervan.
- Strobel, Lee (2000), *The Case for Faith,* Zondervan.

HOUSE CHURCHES AND CELL GROUPS

- Atkerson, Steve, ed. (2003), *Ekklesia: To the Roots of Biblical Church Life,* New Testament Restoration Foundation, www.ntrf.org
- Banks, Robert (1998), *Paul's Idea of Community: The Early House Churches in their Historical Setting,* Eerdmans.
- Birkey, Del (1988), *The House Church,* Herald Press.
- Broadbent, E.H. (1999), *The Pilgrim Church,* Gospel Folio Press.
- Bunton, Peter (2001), *Cell Groups and House Churches: What History Teaches Us,* House to House Publications.
- Comiskey, Joel (1999), *Home Cell Group Explosion,* Touch Publications.
- Driver, John (1999), *Radical Faith: An Alternative History of the Christian Church,* Pandora Press.
- Fitts, Robert (2001), *The Church in the House,* Preparing the Way Publishers (free PDF download from www.robertfitts.com).
- Garrison, David (1999), *Church Planting Movements,* International Mission Board, Southern Baptist Convention, free book download from www.dawnministries.org/general/freedownloads.html

- Kreider, Larry (2001), *House Church Networks*, House-to-House Publications.
- Lund, Robert (2001), *The Way Church Out To Be*, Outside-the-Box Press, www.outside-the-box-press.com
- Rutz, James H., *The Open Church* (see www.openchurch.com).
- Simson, Wolfgang (1998), *Houses that Change the World*, Paternoster Publishing.
- Snyder, C. Arnold (1995), *Anabaptist History and Theology*, Pandora Press.
- Henderson, D.M. (1997), *John Wesley's Class Meeting: A Model for Making Disciples*. Evangel Publishing House.
- Snyder, Howard (1975), *The Problem of Wineskins*, InterVarsity Press.
- Snyder, Howard (1996), *The Radical Wesley and Patterns for Church Renewal*, Wipf and Stock Publishers.
- Viola, Frank (1998), *Rethinking the Wineskin: The Practice of the New Testament Church*, Present Testimony Ministry.
- Viola, Frank (1999), *Who is Your Covering?*, Present Testimony Ministry.
- Viola, Frank (2003), *Pagan Christianity*, Present Testimony Ministry.

WORLD MISSIONS

- Johnstone, P. and J. Mandryk (2001), *Operation World*, WEC International.
- Terry, J.M. et al. (eds.) (1998), *Missiology: An Introduction to the Foundations, History, and Strategies of World Missions*, Broadman and Holman Publishers.
- Winter, R. and S. Hawthorne (eds.) (1981), *Perspectives on the World Christian Movement*, William Carey Library.

WEBSITES

- Canadian House Church Resource Network, www.outreach.ca/cpc/housechurches.htm
- Dove Christian Fellowship International, www.dcfi.org
- Home Church Network, www.homechurch.org
- House Church Canada, www.housechurch.ca
- House-2-House Online Magazine, www.house2house.tv

- New Testament Restoration Foundation, www.ntrf.org
- Open Church Ministries, www.openchurch.com
- Robert Fitts Ministries, www.robertfitts.com

VIDEOS

- *Against Great Odds*, Gateway Films (Box 540, Worcester, PA, USA, 1-800-523-0226), 1992, 29 minutes: documents the growth of Ethiopia's Kristos Church from 5,000 to 50,000 people using underground house churches during ten years of Marxist oppression in the 1980's.

- *Church Planting Movements*, available from International Mission Board of the Southern Baptist Convention (Box 6767, Richmond, VA, USA 23230, 1-800-866-3621, www.imb.org/cpm), 12 minutes: documents rapidly growing church planting movements around the world today that use the multiplication of house churches and/or cell groups of 10-30 people. Accompanies the book by David Garrison of the same title.

APPENDIX 1

COMPARISON CHART OF CHURCH MODELS

The chart contrasts the three classic models of church prevalent today: Traditional Church, Cell Church, and New Testament-style House Churches.

	TRADITIONAL CHURCH	CELL CHURCH	HOUSE CHURCHES
Organizational Principle	Church *WITH* small groups	Church *OF* small groups	Church *IS* small groups
Organizational Diagram	*Hub* Black Circle = Large Group	*Hub and Spokes* Black Dots = Small Groups	*Network* Black Dots = House Churches
Size of Meetings	Large Group with some Small Groups	Equal Emphasis on both Large and Small Groups	Small Groups: Primary HC Network: Supplement
Format of Meetings	Programmed Ritual and Passive Audience	Large Group: Programmed Small Group: Open	Open: Participatory and Interactive
Purpose of Meetings	One-man show	Large Group: One-Man Show Small Group: Mutual Benefit	Mutual Benefit

Comparison Chart of Church Models—Continued

	TRADITIONAL CHURCH	CELL CHURCH	HOUSE CHURCHES
Location of Meetings	Church Building	Large Group: Church Building Small Group: Homes	Homes
Day of Meetings	Sunday	Large Group: Sunday Small Group: Any Day	Sunday and/or Every Day
Duration of Meetings	Fixed (1-2 hours)	Large Group: Usually Fixed Small Group: Flexible	Flexible
Broader Connection	Denomination	Denomination	HC Network
Leadership Structure	Concentrated in One Person	Pyramid Structure & Leader's Ladder	Flat Structure & Leadership Teams

APPENDIX 2

THE EARLY CHURCH AS AN ORGANIZED MOVEMENT

The diagram below shows the indispensable organizational elements that characterized the early church. This pattern of expanding circles of impact was first implemented by the apostles and was carried into many subsequent renewal, reform, and revival movements throughout history. Today's house church movements are strongly encouraged to implement this framework to be as biblical and effective as possible. Note that this is a relatively flat leadership structure, unlike many of the multi-layered pyramid schemes we see in much of the church today.

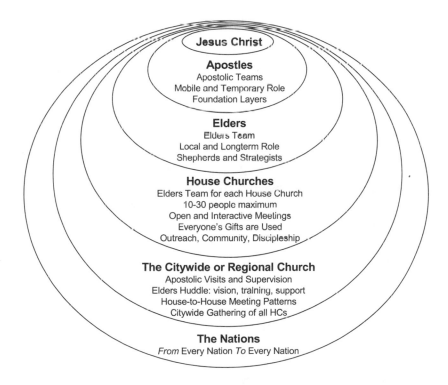

APPENDIX 3

TOP 10 REASONS FOR STARTING HOUSE CHURCHES

The following list is a modified form of one given by Jason Johnston and Rad Zdero in an unpublished manuscript entitled *Save the World...Plant a House Church*. It is available free online in the 'Resources' section at the *House Church Canada* website www.housechurch.ca.

1. **BIBLICAL** – This was the normative New Testament pattern established by Jesus and the apostles and perpetuated by the early church of the first three centuries and in subsequent renewal, reform, and revival movements throughout history.

2. **EXPONENTIAL** – To reach a growing world, we need to multiply, not just add. Current house church movements worldwide are outstripping more traditional church planting and church growth efforts.

3. **EFFECTIVE** – The most effective method of evangelism is not growing existing churches, but planting new ones. House churches are the most easily reproducible form of church and, hence, are the most obvious choice for church planting.

4. **NATURAL** – House churches become part of the local community and easily tap into relationship connections, thereby more readily taking on an indigenous flavour.

5. **PEOPLE FOCUSED** – They focus on relationships and the development of people spiritually, not on executing programs or projects.

6. **EFFICIENT** – They are more mobile, flexible, and adaptable than conventional churches, especially in areas characterized by persecution and poverty.

7. **EQUAL OPPORTUNITY** – Because of their small, intimate, and participatory nature, all believers have the opportunity to exercise their spiritual gifts during church meetings, and not just professional clergy or key leaders.

8. **UNBOUNDED** – They are not limited by church buildings. Whatever use buildings may or may not have, history shows that they are not necessary for rapid church planting movements to start; in fact, they may be a hindrance. Although church buildings are not evil by any means, nor are homes in any way magical, the practical release of time, energy, and money away from building maintenance and into evangelism and discipleship, should cause us to rethink current practices.

9. **INEXPENSIVE** – They are less expensive than traditional church, because no expensive buildings, programs, or professional clergy are required.

10. **IMMEDIATE** – It can start now, right in your living room. There is no need to wait for a gym to be rented or for a building program to be completed to begin a new church or for a full-time pastor to be hired.

APPENDIX 4

FREQUENTLY ASKED QUESTIONS

TRADITIONAL CHURCHES

Q. Are you saying that traditional churches are wrong because they are not house churches?

A. My purpose in writing this book is not to tear down anything that God is doing in and through the traditional church. God has always, is currently, and will continue to use it in drawing people to himself. Of this I have no doubt. It is not my intention at all to throw stones at my brothers and sisters in traditional churches.

However, it must be admitted, traditional churches also perpetuate the unbiblical and often ineffective 'cathedral' model of church, characterized by three cardinal myths that prevent individual believers and the Church as a whole from functioning as strategically and biblically as possible. In essence, the 'cathedral' model of church used by many today is that of a holy man performing a holy ceremony in a holy building. Let's look at each of these points briefly.

The first myth is that of the 'holy man'. Many believe that seminary-trained professional clergy are absolutely indispensable. Biblically, in contrast, the vision of the Church is a priesthood of *all* believers using their talents for building up God's kingdom (1 Pet 2:4-10, 1 Cor 12:7-12,27-30). Make no mistake, there is a biblical pattern of appointed leadership (Mark 3:13-5, Acts 13:1-3, Titus 1:5-9), but this never should result in others believers' talents and skills withering from lack of use, which often happens in conventional churches. In addition, today's single-pastor model stands in contrast to a team of co-equal volunteer elders that managed networks of house churches in the first century (Acts 20:17-21; Titus 1:5).

The second myth is that of the 'holy service'. The very word 'church' for many conjures up images of a few people performing a ritual—however useful or exciting the 'show' may be—in which a few designated individuals perform for a rather passive audience. These gatherings are really one-man shows. Biblical house churches, in contrast, afford open, interactive, and participatory meetings (1

Cor 14:26, Eph 5:19, Col 3:16, Heb 10:25), being an ideal breeding ground for leadership development, every-member participation, and relationship building.

The third myth is that of the 'holy building'. Most people assume that church buildings, or large rented spaces for corporate meetings, are required to be a legitimate church. Whatever church buildings may or may not be useful for, the book of *Acts* and history bear out that they are not requirements for rapid church planting movements, evangelism, or discipleship; in fact, they are often a hindrance. Church buildings also breed a 'temple mentality', which puts church in a box and, thereby, prevents Christians from seeing their very neighbourhoods as mission fields. As well, the massive practical release of time, energy, and money from the elimination of building projects and/or rental payments should challenge us in rethinking current practices.

Today, God is currently ushering in a monumental structural reformation of the global church that addresses these three myths. Cell churches—with their equal emphasis on home cell groups and Sunday morning services in a church building— and house church movements are growing rapidly in non-Western nations and are being used in startling ways to fulfill Christ's Great Commission in this generation. House church movements, though, are even more effective than cell churches in eliminating the above three myths and are closest to the apostolic model of church. Therefore, what I am suggesting is that traditional churches are good, cell churches are better, and house church movements are best. As such, one purpose of this book is to call the church in the West to rethink its approach in light of New Testament practice and strategic effectiveness.

CELL GROUPS

Q. Our church has cell groups. Aren't they basically the same thing as house churches?

A. Many local churches today are implementing all types of small groups, often called 'cell groups', for prayer, crisis support, Bible study, and outreach. This is to be applauded and encouraged.

Traditional churches, however, view these as optional appendages of their church, the main event being the Sunday morning service. A good depiction of this is a bicycle wheel hub with a few spokes. This type of arrangement can be described as a 'church *with* small groups'.

Cell churches, taking things a step further, place an equal emphasis on home cell groups and the Sunday morning service, but still see the cells as the outreach mechanism for the mother church. As well, cell groups are often not fully released by the mother church to function fully as a legitimate church in themselves because they are not allowed to baptize, have the Lord's Supper in their home group, or make important decisions; this is thought to be the sole right of the ordained minister and the board. Even when cell groups are affirmed as where church really happens, this is something that will never sink in for many people because of the ever pervasive 'temple mentality' in traditional churches and even some cell churches; this mindset is almost impossible to change. It is like holding an Alcoholics Anonymous meeting in a bar. Thus, cell churches function like a bicycle wheel hub of many spokes and can be explained as a 'church *of* small groups'.

New Testament-style house churches, on the other hand, are churches in and of themselves and do not belong to a mother 'cathedral' church, although they may (and should) be part of a tight spider web or network of house churches that plans, prays, and plays together. These networks function using the organizational principle that 'church *is* small groups'.

FOLLOWING APOSTOLIC PATTERNS TODAY

Q. Do we have to follow the apostolic church patterns of the New Testament for today?

A. It is clear that the apostles expected believers to follow their lead. Whether we choose to do so today depends on how we view the authority of the apostles and what we make of their expectations that churches would pay attention to what they said and did.

Does this imply blindly following the New Testament, without considering its cultural context and ours? Certainly not. Apostolic directives concerned church patterns, not cultural ones. In other words, this does not mean we need to wear togas and sandals, ride donkeys into town as we eat dried fruit and fish, anoint our hair with oil, and forbid the use of modern technology. But, it *does* mean we are to follow their example and instructions regarding church meeting formats, the relationship between churches, how leaders are appointed, how leaders are to function, etc., because of the nature of what God designed the church to *be* and what he designed it to *do*.

Now, it is true that many churches today do follow *some* of the apostolic patterns observed in the New Testament. However, they stop short of adopting all of them. The argument being made here is for consistency. If churches adopt apostolic beliefs (orthodoxy), then why not adopt apostolic practices (orthopraxy) as well? And, if *some* apostolic practices are already being implemented, then why not go the whole way and incorporate *all* of them?

The great irony is that Christians have spent the last 1700 years basically debating which alternative to apostolic practice should be followed and yet have missed the point: the apostolic blueprint itself should be the norm for the church. The real question should not be 'Do we have to follow New Testament patterns today?' but, rather, 'Why would we want to do it any other way?'

FORM AND FUNCTION IN THE EARLY CHURCH

Q. Isn't it okay for us to simply apply New Testament guidelines today without being worried about whether we do things exactly the way they did in the first century? Isn't "function" more important than "form"? After all, hasn't the church "evolved" over time to adapt to new circumstances, anyway?

A. This idea is an appealing one on a gut level for many. Most Christians today tend to hold this view. The basic argument is that "function" is more important than "form" and, if we can discern the guiding principles of function in the New Testament, then the form does not matter. We are free to "evolve" the "forms" of church today to new unfolding circumstances as long as "function" is maintained. There are two major problems with this line of reasoning.

First, *form and function cannot be separated; they are forever linked together.* If the form of something is changed, this will automatically alter its function and/or its efficiency in performing that function. Consider, for example, the person who has an accident and loses a thumb. The form of their hand has changed from five fingers to four. The function of grasping objects now has forever been altered. To be sure, the person can undergo rehabilitation therapy and adapt their four fingers to grasp objects in a new way. However, although some of the grasping function still remains, the disfigured hand does not function anywhere nearly as effectively as it did with a thumb. The same can be said of the church. God designed the church with certain form-function relationships; he designed it a certain way in order to do a certain thing. If we alter the forms using our human wisdom and understanding, then we can potentially be preventing the church from being what it is meant to be and doing what it is meant to do.

Second, *the evolutionary theory of the church can and has been used to rationalize and justify all sorts of departures from scripture in teaching and practice.* If we are free to "evolve" the church, then there is nothing wrong at all with infant baptism, enforced celibacy for clergy, multi-layered hierarchical leadership, state-church mergers, praying to dead saints, etc. If the ultimate authority for the church is *not* apostolic practice and teaching as revealed in the scriptures, then we are free to do what is right in our own eyes and no scriptural argument whatsoever can be made to address any of these or other issues, including moral ones. Fortunately, many renewal, reform, and revival movements throughout church history were brave enough to address some serious departures from apostolic practice and teaching and sought to steer the church back on the right track. The Waldensians and Methodists brought back a church for and run by lay people, rather than being clergy dominated. The Anabaptists brought voluntary, adult, believer's baptism back to the church. The Quakers brought back personal devotion to Christ and open Spirit-led church meetings. We owe much to these and other groups and individuals for reminding us of the New Testament way. However, much still remains even in the evangelical and charismatic church of today that needs to be renewed and reformed if we are to be as biblical and effective as possible.

LEADERSHIP TRAINING AND QUALIFICATIONS

Q. How are house church leaders trained? Who makes sure they are qualified and ready?

A. Three elements of training can be implemented to see the emergence of highly qualified house church leaders, whether they are local workers or are traveling apostolic type workers.

The *apprenticeship approach*, which is the most effective method, is described in the book as M.A.W.L. (Model, Assist, Watch, and Leave). Mentors work closely alongside their mentorees who are constantly observing and assisting. Leaders-in-progress also take on independent practical hands-on assignments and report back to their coach for debriefing. Both Jesus and Paul employed this model.

The *leaders huddle* method is described earlier in the book as 4D (Dream-Drill-Discuss-Dinner). Leaders of a house church network gather together regularly, say once or twice monthly, for a time of teaching, planning, praying, resourcing, accountability, and eating. In this context, there may be a more experienced and mature leader facilitating the learning process for the group, in addition to the mutual learning that takes place.

The *formal seminary* route also has its place. It is important to have at least a few individuals who have taken theology courses and/or have earned degrees in theology involved in the house church movement. These folks will provide some of the necessary academic tools to ensure both theological breadth and depth. However, the capability of so called lay people to become self-taught and very knowledgeable should not be underestimated.

ACCOUNTABILITY

Q. Isn't there a danger of house churches going off track theologically and behaviourally? How are they to be held accountable?

A. There is a valid concern about independent groups becoming cults or sects, either behaviourally or doctrinally. History has shown this can happen. On the other hand, some of the most organized and structured religious bodies in the world today also propagate some of the most serious distortions of New Testament faith and practice, namely the Mormons, Jehovah's Witnesses, and the Roman Catholic Church.

The lesson here is that human control and accountability do not necessarily eliminate doctrinal or behavioral problems. There are many local churches today, in fact, that are independent but are within the mainstream of evangelical Christianity. They act as self-regulating bodies. Denominations and mission groups, for the most part, also act as self-regulating bodies. Therefore, autonomy in itself does not necessarily lead to wrong beliefs and bad behaviour.

Even so, it is strongly recommended that house churches become part of house church networks for mutual accountability. Leaders voluntarily and mutually submit for scrutiny both their personal lives and ministries. These networks also have the advantage of the partnership and synergy that comes from working closely alongside others. The role of apostles, too, is of great importance; we need people who have calling, character, and competence to circulate among house churches from time to time and coach them to greater health and vitality.

DENOMINATIONS

Q. Should house church movements be part of denominations?

A. This author's opinion is that denominations are not God's ideal for the Church. The only legitimate biblical reason for division in the Body of Christ—apart from doctrinal issues—is geographical distance. Thus, the early Church had a theology of unity and utilized a citywide (or regional) church model. Even so, today's reality is that we do have denominations.

What, then, should a house church do? This is a matter of some disagreement among those involved in the movement. Some are opposed to the idea for theological and practical reasons. Others are in favour of it because of the accountability and support provided by denominations.

The advantages of participating in a denomination include an increased legitimacy of house churches in the eyes both of Christians and the broader culture, accountability regarding doctrine and behaviour, financial and resource support, and an opportunity for educating other Christians about house churches.

The disadvantage, which is significant, is that of potential denominational interference or undue control in the local activities of house churches, especially when it comes to administration of the Lord's Supper and Baptism, leadership development, and financial decisions.

Therefore, this author neither encourages nor discourages house churches from participating in a denomination, leaving it up to the conscience and circumstances of individuals.

CHILDREN

Q. What about children in house churches?

A. One of the most important topics, especially for parents, is whether a house church can truly meet the needs of children. There are basically three possible approaches, namely integration, specialization, and parental apprenticeship.

Integration means that some house churches try to fully incorporate children into the meetings. In this way church gatherings function like multi-generational family gatherings.

S*pecialization* refers to having a separate time for the young ones in another part of the home that is focused on meeting their specific needs. In addition, a network of home churches may band together to have some specialized occasional programming for children and even young teens. In the case of older teens or those going about to step into college or university, a house church can be completely comprised of and led by young people, with the support and accountability of their house church network.

Parental apprenticeship refers to the primary responsibility of Christian parents—more than anyone else—to raise their children in the Lord during the natural daily activities of family life, rather than relying predominantly on specialist youth workers within whatever type of church. For better or worse, young people often grow up mimicking the beliefs and behaviors of their parents, which should be a challenge to moms and dads to live their Christianity out in front of their kids.

WEDDINGS

Q. How would wedding ceremonies work in house churches? What about the legal implications?

A. In most traditional church settings, an ordained priest or minister has the authority from both their denomination and the state to perform wedding ceremonies. If house church networks are truly to be seen as genuine Christian communities, they must also be given the opportunity to validate and witness—before God—the joining of a woman and man in marriage. Several creative options are available to house churches that can meet both spiritual and legal obligations.

First, the happy couple can arrange to have a Christian wedding officiated by their home church elder(s), apostolic leader(s), or other person in a hall, backyard, or other setting of their choice. This would be followed by a brief separate civil ceremony at city hall to meet government requirements.

Second, if there happens to be someone in a home church network that is an ordained minister or who has a license to perform weddings, then only one ceremony would be necessary.

Money Matters

Q. How do money matters work themselves out in house church networks?

A. As with the issue of denominations, there are different practices among house churches concerning church bank accounts, tax deductible donations, and tithing. There are advantages and disadvantages to each of these items. Some house churches do not incorporate any of these elements, but rather use money solely for mutual support within the house church as the need arises and in assisting the poor. Money, thus, flows directly from giver to getter, and bypasses middle agencies like the government and denominational finance departments. Others incorporate all three elements and, in that way, function like traditional churches, except that the money is not spent on expensive programs, paying rent or paying for the church building program, or supporting professional clergy. Instead, they funnel their money to the poor, for resources to be used within the house church and/or network, and in the support of house church planters and mobile network overseers. There are also house churches that fall somewhere between these two ends of the finance management spectrum. So, I recommend that money matters be left to individual house churches and/or networks to work out.

Overseas Missions and Mercy Ministries

Q. How can a small house church be involved in financing missionaries and poverty relief efforts?

A. Conventional churches can spend up to 80% of their budget simply on supporting their full time clergy person and paying off the mortgage for the church building. Individual house churches, on the other hand, do not have either of these expenses. House church networks, though, sometimes partially or fully support apostolic house church planters and/or those who provide coaching. Nevertheless, strictly speaking, a house church grouping with an equivalent number of people as a single conventional congregation has significantly more financial leverage in supporting overseas missionaries, relief organizations, and local mercy ministries.

ABOUT THE AUTHOR

Rad Zdero earned his Ph.D. degree in Mechanical Engineering from Queen's University in Kingston, Canada, specializing in orthopaedic biomechanics and prosthesis design. He is currently the research director of a hospital-based orthopaedic research lab. For the past 18 years he has also participated in, led, and started alternative, grassroots, Christian communities called "cell groups" and "house-churches" with the Navigators and Campus Crusade for Christ, as well as in a traditional church context. He is currently involved with *House Church Canada*—an affiliate of The Free Methodist Church in Canada—which is a team of people dedicated to developing a network of house-churches in the greater Toronto area. He enjoys long walks, epic movies, books, writing poetry and music, and coffee shops.

MAKE CONTACT

If you are interested in discussing house-churches further or would like to partner with *House Church Canada* in starting a house-church network in your area, feel free to contact the author. He would enjoy hearing from you.

Rad Zdero
P.O. Box 39528
Lakeshore P.O.
Mississauga, ON
Canada L5G-4S6

Website: www.housechurch.ca
Email: rad@housechurch.ca